Isn't It
Their Turn to
Pick Up the Check?

Dealing with All of the

Trickiest Money Problems Between Family

and Friends—from Serial Borrowers

to Serious Cheapskates

Jeanne Fleming, Ph.D., and Leonard Schwarz

FREE PRESS
New York London Toronto Sydney

Note to Readers:
Names of and identifying details about the people who
told the authors their stories have been changed,
as have the names of and identifying details about
the people in these stories.

*f*P
Free Press
A Division of Simon & Schuster, Inc.
1230 Avenue of the Americas
New York, NY 10020

Copyright © 2008 by Jeanne Fleming and Leonard Schwarz

First Free Press hardcover edition January 2008

FREE PRESS and colophon are trademarks of Simon & Schuster, Inc.

For information about special discounts for bulk purchases, please contact
Simon & Schuster Special Sales at
1-800-456-6798 or business@simonandschuster.com

Designed by Katy Riegel

Some material in this book was previously published in articles by the authors
that appeared in their "Do the Right Thing" column in *Money Magazine* and/or
on the CNNMoney.com website. © 2004–2007 Time Inc.

Manufactured in the United States of America

1 3 5 7 9 10 8 6 4 2

Library of Congress Cataloging-in-Publication Data
Fleming, Jeanne. Isn't it *their* turn to pick up the check?: dealing with all of the
trickiest money problems between family and friends—from serial borrowers to
serious cheapskates / Jeanne Fleming and Leonard Schwarz.
p. cm.
1. Money—Social aspects.   2. Interpersonal relations—Economic aspects.
3. Family—Economic aspects.   4. Inheritance and succession—Social aspects.
5. Money—Psychological aspects.   I. Schwarz, Leonard.   II. Title.   III. Title:
Money problems between family and friends.
HG221.F63 2008
332.024—dc22   2007023458
ISBN-13: 978-1-4165-4200-1
ISBN-10: 1-4165-4200-0

Contents

I'll Take the Flu

WHICH WOULD YOU rather have: a relative ask you for a large loan, or a bad case of the flu?

We asked this question of eight hundred people in a national survey, and you can probably guess what over two-thirds of them said: I'll take the flu.

This book is about what to do when you can't choose the flu.

Consider it a handbook for the awkward moments and uncomfortable situations that the intersection of money and personal relationships so often gives rise to. It's about dealing with the brother-in-law you haven't heard from since you lent him money and the nephew who always has his hand out, about friends who never pick up a check and neighbors who always need your car.

Of course, not every money-and-relationships problem is created by a mooch, freeloader, deadbeat, or other ethically challenged individual. An elderly parent's ill-conceived will can turn even the closest brother and sister against one another. Disparities in wealth can create trying moments for the best of friends. And differences in perspective or expectation can lead honorable people to fiercely disagree about the ethical way to respond to a difficult situation.

Once upon a time it was sex that people felt uncomfortable discussing, but today it's money. Not Warren Buffett's money, or the money your neighbor got for his home, or the money it cost to take your kids to a ball game. It's the money problems you experience with friends and family— problems you hate to mention for fear of sounding judgmental or just plain small, problems you're slow to raise because you think a confrontation could be in the cards. It's the forty bucks that your friend borrowed the last time you went out and that she's never offered to repay. It's your cheapskate brother showing up for Thanksgiving dinner with a single bottle of six-dollar wine. And it's the additional money you worry your friends think you should have spent on their wedding present, even though you feel you've spent more than enough.

With his research, Alfred Kinsey revealed how utterly commonplace so many sexual practices and worries were to a world in which they were never discussed. We're no Kinsey, but we have conducted a couple of surveys in unplowed fields ourselves—one for *Money Magazine* and one exclusively for this book. Together, they illuminate how ubiquitous moochers, deadbeats, cheapskates, and their like are and document just how much trouble these folks cause. Where Kinsey determined the percentage of Americans who said they engaged in extramarital sex, we can tell you how many people say they've got a freeloader in their family. And being, we admit, more judgmental than Kinsey, we're prepared to tell you what to do about the bum.

But what if the money-and-relationship problem keeping you awake at night isn't the fault of the greedy or the selfish? What if the sticky situation you're facing originates from a will; from a misunderstanding over a loan; or from a promise, made with the best of intentions, that now appears impossible to keep? Again, we have research that reveals the prevalence of the problem you're facing. And again, we're prepared to help you solve it—to tell you how to deal with the mess created by that will, loan, or promise.

For the record, we are for honesty, generosity, kindness, and respect. But we are also for speaking up, drawing lines, and not allowing yourself to be taken advantage of. We believe there is nothing wrong with caring about money and everything wrong with pretending not to care about money—especially when it's other people's.

Reading our book won't make your nephew who wants your money and your neighbor who wants your car disappear. But what it will do is give you enough ammunition—enough moral support—so that, when money-and-relationship troubles darken your door, you won't feel like you'd rather have the flu.

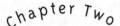

Chapter Two

Take My Relatives, Please!

Happiness is having a large, loving, caring,
close-knit family in another city.

—George Burns

WE HAVEN'T COME across any research to this effect, but we'd be willing to bet that, when Neanderthals roamed Northern Europe, there were always a couple of guys on the hunt who inevitably grabbed the choicest cuts of reindeer and acted as if they hadn't taken anything special. We'd also bet that each tribe had a guy who was always quick to consume his own berries, then kept asking others if they wanted all of theirs. And finally we'd bet that every Neanderthal at some point had to deal with a friend who borrowed his best spear, returned it with the tip chipped, and said "What could I do? My son was playing with it, and you know how kids are."

Perhaps a few of these characters got the clubbing they deserved, but their genes most definitely survived. Listen to people today talk about their big family holiday dinner and, no matter how wonderful it was, you still hear about the aunt who went cheap on presents for the kids, the sister who thinks bringing pies exempts her from helping in the kitchen, and the brother-in-law who single-handedly drank all the hosts' good Scotch—a fifteen-year-old single malt that he would never dream of buying for himself.

Every family today includes some otherwise perfectly fine people who are simply off when it comes to money matters. While most of us try to rise above our relatives' flaws, that can be tough to do. Your resentment grows, your wallet suffers, and—having not been confronted on his or her bad behavior—your relative continues to misbehave.

If there's good news here, it's that you're not alone—everyone has a couple of thoughtless or selfish relatives. Meet a few of the classics.

∾

My brother bought a new car instead of repaying the loan I gave him.

When a relative cheats on your kindness

Question: A year ago, I lent one of my younger brothers $3,500 when his employer went bankrupt. Josh agreed to pay me $150 a month until the loan was paid off, and he has never been late with a payment. But six months ago Josh landed a well-paying new job, and last weekend he arrived at our parents' thirty-fifth-anniversary barbecue in a brand new SUV.

My husband is furious. He feels that Josh should have paid me what he owed me rather than use my no-interest loan to help buy a car that happens to be a lot nicer than mine. I, too, wish my brother had paid me back before buying an expensive car. But since he's never missed a payment, I don't think Josh has really done anything wrong. Has he?

Answer: While your brother has lived up to the letter of your agreement with him, he has ignored the spirit of generosity in which the loan was made. You lent him $3,500 in his hour of need, not asking for security and not asking for interest. In return, your brother should pay you back at the earliest date he reasonably can, not at the latest date his agreement with you permits.

Normally it's tough to find fault with someone who is faithfully paying off a debt as promised. But your brother wants to have it both ways. When he needed help—when he needed an unsecured, interest-free, four-figure loan— Josh turned to you as family. But now that he's back in the chips, your brother is treating the loan as if it came from a bank.

For that reason, your husband's not wrong to be upset. If Josh had a better moral compass, he'd have repaid the balance of his debt to you before buying that new set of wheels. At the very least, he should have spoken to you about his intentions before buying the SUV.

Do him a favor. Tell him where he went wrong. Being clueless may get Josh off the hook with his big sister. But most of the people he is going to deal with in life are likely to react to his self-centeredness just as your husband did.

My sister sold Mom's engagement ring on eBay.

When someone sells a family treasure

Question: When my mother died, she left her very beautiful engagement ring to my sister. Carol, who didn't particularly care for the ring and who prides herself on being unsentimental about family, promptly sold it on eBay. My other sister and I are heartsick about this. Since the ring was a family heirloom, didn't she owe it to us to first ask us if we wanted it?

Answer: You bet.

It's sad but true: Parents now and then leave a family treasure to precisely the person who will value it least. Sometimes the reason is simple ("She's the oldest daughter, so she should have it"). Sometimes it's more complex ("Maybe this will make her feel more connected to her heritage—and to me").

Folks like your sister, who couldn't care less about family items, have no ethical obligation to refuse such a bequest. But common decency dictates that, before disposing of an heirloom, they offer other members of their family an opportunity to buy it or trade for it. (The same holds true for heirs who simply need money a lot more than they need whatever family treasure they've inherited.)

Your sister behaved badly in disposing of the engagement ring the way she did. If you're thinking it was meant to be a slap in the face to her mother—and to you and your sister as well—we think you may be right.

◦— **NOBODY'S PERFECT** —◦

We meant it when we said that everyone has at least a few relatives who are simply off when it comes to money matters. Here's the proof:

We asked the participants in our survey whether—among their friends and relatives—there were any cheapskates, corner cutters, moochers, freeloaders, and the like. Here's what they had to say.

	PERCENT WHO SAY:	
TYPE OF PERSON	AT LEAST ONE FAMILY MEMBER IS	AT LEAST ONE FRIEND IS
Cheapskate	49%	42%
User (person who takes advantage of others)	45%	35%
Corner cutter	42%	37%
Greedy in his or her dealings	40%	29%
Dishonest in his or her dealings	38%	26%
Moocher	36%	32%
Freeloader	35%	26%
Deadbeat	35%	22%

Source: Fleming & Schwarz survey.   *(continued)*

So if you've ever wondered whether you're the only one who has to deal with a brother-in-law who always sticks you with the tab, a cousin who never repays a loan, or a friend who never refills the gas tank when he uses your car, wonder no more. These guys are everywhere.

Must I give my misguided brother investment advice he needs but doesn't want to hear?

When a family member is about to do something stupid

Question: My brother, a successful dentist who fancies himself a hotshot investor, recently bragged that he's about to buy a large parcel of undeveloped land. I'm a CPA, and I happen to know a bit about investing in raw land. I also know that my brother has no idea of the risks associated with this type of investment—in particular, how illiquid it is. Am I obligated to tell him, even though I'm sure the last thing in the world he wants to hear is his big sister warning him, yet again, that he's being foolish?

Answer: Why is it such a thankless task, saving the people we love from their own worst impulses? Fortunately, we're rarely obligated to do so. Your brother's an adult, and adults are entitled to make their own decisions and their own mistakes. In fact, once they both grow up, big sisters need to let their little brothers do just that. Only two circumstances obligate you to give your brother your opinion: if he asks for it, or if you think he's about to seriously jeopardize his family's financial resources.

Obviously you're off the hook on the first count. So unless you're worried a genuine calamity is about to occur—unless your brother tells you he's betting the ranch on this one, or your sister-in-law turns pale each time he brings it up—you can in good conscience keep your advice to yourself.

And who knows? Maybe if you withhold your opinion, your brother will find himself missing your good counsel instead of resenting it.

⌐— SHOULD YOU OR SHOULDN'T YOU? —⌐

Fifty-four percent of the public agree with the statement:

"You should never give financial advice to a relative."

Source: Fleming & Schwarz survey.

The older you are, the more likely you are to agree. Meaning, we'd argue, that younger folks don't fully appreciate how many second-guessers and finger-pointers life has in store for them.

My sister's husband wants a piece of my profits.

When a family member wants you to pay him for a stock tip

Question: I recently made $2,500 on a stock I bought on my brother-in-law Jack's recommendation. Jack works for an ad agency, and everyone there is excited about this company's new product, for which they're developing a campaign. Jack didn't buy any stock himself, because he and my sister are saving to make a down payment on a house. But now, ever since I told him about my big hit, he keeps asking for his "cut." Do I owe him one?

Answer: First of all, we're assuming Jack did not provide you with what the authorities consider to be inside information. (If he did, it's a trifle late to be writing us. You should be contacting a lawyer.)

That issue aside, if Jack liked the stock so much, he should have bought some himself. To be sure, he'd be risking the family nest egg. But that's how you make money in the stock market: by taking a risk—not by deciding you can't afford to while staking a claim to a piece of the profits of someone who did.

Which isn't to criticize Jack for playing it safe. On the contrary, saving for a home is a wise thing to do. But since you alone put up the money and you alone took the risk of losing it, you alone are entitled to the profit.

While Jack is wrong to expect a cut, he does deserve your thanks. To show your appreciation, you should take him to a ball game or buy him a couple of bottles of nice wine. And if he continues to pester you for that cut, ask Jack what percent of your losses he was prepared to make up had the stock gone south.

My mother is blowing my inheritance.

When your mother makes generous gifts to charity rather than
preserving her estate for the family

Question: My father was a successful surgeon, and, when
he died, he left my mother several million dollars plus a
beautiful home, worth millions more. He also left my
brother and me $50,000 each, which seemed fine at the
time because we knew that we and our children were
Mom's only beneficiaries.

In recent years, however, my mother has become very
involved with an environmental group and has begun giving them gobs of money. Last year alone she contributed
$250,000.

While I'm sympathetic to the causes she's supporting,
I think she's being irresponsible in spending Dad's money
so freely. Shouldn't she be as concerned with her sons' and
her grandchildren's economic futures as she is with the
rainforest?

Answer: What? You don't want to take your family down to
Brazil some day to see the fruit of your mother's generosity
and to polish the plaque that honors the millions of dollars
that went to the rainforest instead of to you?

Seriously, we can understand your horror as you watch
a small fortune you thought would be yours steadily erode.
But the simple truth is: It's your mother's money to do with
more or less as she pleases.

We're guessing you would have mentioned it if you or

your brother were facing some economic hardship or if your mother were giving money away at a rate that threatened to make her financially dependent on you. But assuming neither to be the case, your mother is doing nothing wrong in spending her money as she sees fit.

Everything changes, though, if your father left the bulk of his estate to your mother with the understanding that she would pass it on to you, your brother, and your children. Even if he never put anything in writing, your mother has an obligation to honor the wishes she knows were in his heart when he left her his money.

⌒ SOME GUYS HAVE ALL THE LUCK ⌒

Only one person in three says they've never had a problem involving money with a close friend or relative.

Source: Fleming & Schwarz survey.

All my brother gave our child for Christmas was a lousy comic book.

When there's a serious cheapskate in the family

Question: My brother is a terrible cheapskate. Just for example, he gave my son a two-dollar comic book for Christmas again this year (we always give his kids nice presents). And I wound up paying for most of our father's sixty-fifth birthday party because my brother claimed many of the expenses, like nice wine, were unnecessary. It's not as if he is poor, by the way. He has just as much money as my husband and I do.

I've told my brother his penny-pinching is unfair to other people, and he's told me the way he spends his money is none of my business. Who's right?

Answer: That depends. Is your brother truly a cheapskate or merely a tightwad?

Here's what we mean. Your brother isn't required to spend his money on more expensive gifts, more expensive wines, or anything else just because that's what you'd prefer. And that's true whether he's Donald Trump or Donald Trump's driver.

There's a big difference, though, between being tight with money and failing to spend what an occasion calls for. If your brother was unwilling to pony up for his share of the food and drink that others in your family agreed would be customary for your father's party, then he's a cheapskate. And if that's the case, it *is* your business. You have every right to protest and every right to insist on being reimbursed.

Now about those nice presents you've been giving your brother's kids: Has he happily accepted them and said nothing, or has he let you know he thought they were extravagant? If he's said nothing, you again have a right to complain. Because unless he's told you he doesn't want to exchange expensive gifts, your brother has no business reaping the benefits of your willingness to do what he won't—spend money on other people.

Our son and his wife spend money like it's going
out of style.

When an adult child relies on his parents to bail out his family

Question: Our only child, Christopher, is a real estate agent, and his wife Nicole is a designer for a textile firm. Together they make a good living, but they spend every last cent of it and then some. They're always going out to expensive restaurants, leasing luxury cars, and vacationing at the newest, most expensive resorts. And they also keep asking my husband and me to help with their bills.

Last week Christopher called to say he was short on cash and to ask if we could let him have $1,500 to buy our grandchildren the computers they need for school. Before that, he needed $600 for "unexpected medical bills" when the copayment changed on Nicole's health insurance. And before that, it was the children's orthodontist. Every few months it's something.

My husband and I love our son and his family, and, fortunately, we can afford to help them. But I think we should stop. Christopher and Nicole need to learn to live within their means, and they never will if we keep bailing them out. My husband disagrees. He says that ultimately Christopher and his family are going to inherit everything we have, so what's the harm in advancing them a few thousand dollars every year. And he also makes the point that our grandchildren—like all children today—need computers, and that it isn't fair to punish them for their parents' failings.

What should we do?

Answer: As annoying and disheartening as we're sure it must be to have Christopher and Nicole constantly hitting you up for cash, their always outstretched hands are the least of your problems. Your son and daughter-in-law appear to be completely irresponsible spendthrifts, and their imprudent ways have serious long-term implications.

Specifically: How long do you think it will take them to burn through the money you're planning to leave them? And once they do, who's going to help out your grandchildren, whether it's with new computers, their college education, or the down payment on a home?

As you say, you can afford to give Christopher the money he's asked for, and as your husband says, kids need computers. So the answer to your specific question is simple: Hold your nose and write the check.

But to solve the real problem here, you should have a lawyer prepare new wills for you and your husband—wills that provide for two things: (1) that your son and daughter-in-law get a monthly, quarterly, or annual stipend, but that they don't have access to the principal of your estate; and (2) that your grandchildren have access to the principal when they need it or are old enough to handle it responsibly (how's age thirty sound?).

There are several ways to accomplish this, and a good attorney will have no trouble devising a plan that addresses your concerns and your grandchildren's needs.

As for Christopher and Nicole, we wish we could be more encouraging. But frankly, we think they've gone well past the point where a little tough love will straighten them out. Leopards don't change their spots—and neither do middle-aged fat cats.

⚬— WHEN THE CHIPS ARE DOWN —⚬

Who do people say they trust to handle their finances if they die or become incapacitated?

Spouse or partner	46%
Parent	17%
Child	14%
Brother or sister	9%
Friend	2%
Lawyer	2%
Financial adviser	2%
Someone else	1%
No one	2%

Source: *Wall Street Journal* Online/Harris Interactive Personal Finance Poll.

All the problems they have with relatives notwithstanding, who do people trust when the chips are down? Family, family, family.

Chapter Three

Borrowers and Lenders Behaving Badly

Borrow money from a pessimist. They don't expect it back.

—Anonymous

RYAN IS A charming but completely irresponsible twenty-five-year-old who is always borrowing money from his doting Aunt Charlotte. He's either short on the rent or has lost his BlackBerry or needs to have his car repaired. With Ryan, it's always something.

Recently, Charlotte gave Ryan a much more substantial loan than usual—$1,800—so he could pay off his credit cards and "get a new start." A week later, her neighbor saw Ryan and his girlfriend at a pricey restaurant of the sort that frugal Charlotte wouldn't be caught dead in. When the neighbor mentioned this to Charlotte, Charlotte told her "Honey, if he enjoys spending my money as much as I've enjoyed saving it, I'll be a very happy woman."

Rare is the creditor who shares Charlotte's sunny perspective. Search the Internet for famous quotations about borrowing and lending, and what you'll find is centuries worth of knowing cynicism. Our favorite: Benjamin Franklin's wry observation that "Creditors have better memories than debtors."

According to the Federal Reserve Board's Survey of Consumer Finances, there are several billion dollars in loans outstanding between friends and family members in this country. An optimist would say this shows just how much we trust one another. A pessimist would say that's a lot of trouble waiting to happen.

~

My girlfriend's brother always has his hand out.

When someone keeps asking for more

Question: My girlfriend's brother is constantly complaining about how poor he is and then hitting her up for cash, which she never sees again. Two examples: He borrowed $1,500 from her eight months ago and hasn't paid any of it back. And when he came by to see her the other day, he left his car insurance bill on our kitchen table for her to pay. The guy works, at least most of time, but his wife sits home all day and smokes Marlboros at five bucks a pack. Right now my girlfriend's sisters want her to chip in with them to help pay his rent. What should she do?

Answer: Move. No kidding, move. Many of your girlfriend's problems would go away if it weren't so easy for her brother and sisters to drop in and pressure her to part with her money.

Somehow your girlfriend's brother has convinced his family that they need to take care of him. We'd bet that when they were kids, the same pattern existed—that when their brother blew his allowance on day one, the sisters would treat him to ice cream the rest of the week.

But being indulged as a child is no excuse for being irresponsible as an adult. Your girlfriend's brother is systematically taking advantage of her weak willpower and strong sense of loyalty, and that's unethical. One way to deal with this problem is to make it more difficult for him to ask her for money (that's the "move" strategy). The only other way is for your girlfriend to learn to say no—no to him and no to his emissaries. While saying no can be tough to do, professional help exists for learning how to do it, plus your girlfriend has you to lean on when the going gets rough.

Good luck to both of you. And a word of caution: Whatever you do, don't mingle your finances with your girlfriend's until she solves this problem.

⌒— **BORROWING TROUBLE** —⌒

Two-thirds of the public—68 percent to be precise—say they've experienced trouble with friends or family members in the process of borrowing or lending money.
What's more, about one-quarter of these folks say they've experienced a lot of trouble.

Source: *Money* survey.

Angry because a good friend ignores your requests to be repaid? Feeling guilty because your sister wants a loan and you don't want to lend her the money? At least you can relax on one score: You have a lot of company.

My friend's wife won't let him help me out.

When a friend you've lent money to won't lend money to you

Question: When I was in college, I lent $2,500 to my friend Nick, who needed the money to be able to stay in school. Later, when we both got good IT jobs, I told him to forget about the loan. A few months ago, though, I lost my job. When I asked Nick, who's doing well, for a $5,000 loan so I could get by for a while, he said he'd like to help, but he's married now and his wife's against it. This doesn't seem fair. Is it?

Answer: No, it isn't. When two people get married, each of them brings to the marriage lots of things that will play a role in their shared financial future. Some things are assets—things like the bride's wealthy uncle, the groom's parents' vacation home, and the bride's newly minted degree from Cornell's medical school. And some are liabilities, like the bride's student loans, the groom's looming orthodonture bill, and the bride's alcoholic father who can't hold a job.

In the case of your friend Nick, one asset he brought to his marriage was you—a buddy with a good heart. And one liability he brought was the obligation he incurred when he accepted $2,500 from you, namely: the obligation to help you out should you be the one in need.

What Nick fails to grasp is that marriage, in general— and the objections of a spouse, in particular—don't allow you to shuck off your obligations to others. While there may be good reasons why he is unable to lend you money right now, "my wife won't let me" isn't one of them.

My mother likes to brag about how much she's lent me.

When someone reveals to others that he or she has lent you money

Question: My mother has always been very generous with me. When I got married, she lent my wife and me the money for the down payment on our home—a loan I repaid in full. Since then, Mom has given me several other loans, most of which I repaid, though several were forgiven at her insistence.

I'm forty-five now and appreciative of all my mother

has done. But in recent years, Mom has begun bragging about her generosity to my wife and me, and it makes us feel small. For example, at family gatherings, she always finds an occasion to say things like "It was my pleasure to see that they could buy a house," or "When their children went to music camp, you know who wrote the check." I know Mom isn't trying to humiliate us, but her behavior has that effect. What do you think? Is it ethical to talk so openly about the financial help you've given people—especially members of your own family?

Answer: Some mothers can never seem to stop talking about their children.

Seriously, an individual who lends money has an obligation to show respect for the person to whom she's lent the money, and one dimension of showing respect is being discreet. In making her generosity to you a frequent topic of conversation, your mother is indulging herself at your expense, and that's wrong. The fact that she's unaware of what she's doing doesn't get her off the hook. It's never okay to make others feel small.

This said, it wouldn't necessarily be wrong for your mother to confide, say, in a sibling that she's lent you money—or to confide in one of yours, if there are any. Unless their having this information would be to your detriment or unless you've specifically asked your mother not to mention the loans and gifts and she's agreed, she has every right to speak—with discretion—about her generosity. In other words, the ethical line she's crossed has to do with speaking too publicly about your financial affairs and humiliating you in the process. But the fact that she lent you money is not, in and of itself, a secret your mother is obligated to take to her grave.

⌒— BROTHER, CAN YOU SPARE A DIME? —⌒

How much money do people borrow from one another? Here, from our *Money* survey, are the responses to the question: "What's the largest amount of money you've ever borrowed from a friend or family member?"

	PERCENT WHO ANSWERED
$0	21%
$1–$100	18%
$101–$500	17%
$501–$1,000	10%
$1,001–$5,000	24%
$5,001–$10,000	5%
$10,001–$19,999	2%
$20,000 or more	3%

Source: *Money* survey.

With one person in three borrowing $1,000 or more at least once, you can see how central the Bank of Friends & Family is in our lives.

My brother thinks he's Warren Buffett.

When you ask for a loan and you get a lecture

Question: I recently asked my brother to lend me several thousand dollars, to which he said no. That's okay with me. But what wasn't okay is that he took the opportunity to lecture me on my "ridiculously extravagant lifestyle" and to preach about how it was "time for me to learn how to save." Does my asking him for money really give him the right to speak to me that way? I'm no kid, by the way, and it's not as if my brother's an accountant or some other kind of financial professional. The guy works at the post office.

Answer: Ouch! What a treat that dressing down must have been for you.

Unless you've left something important out of the picture here—unless, say, this is the tenth time you've asked him for money—your brother was way out of line. Whatever he may think, and however right or wrong he may be, it was unfair for him to use the fact that you'd asked for a loan to scold you like that. Any polite request for help—whether from a family member, a charity, or a homeless person—merits a more respectful response.

Though your brother was wrong to berate you, he wasn't out of line in offering you some unsolicited advice. By asking him for money, you put your finances on the table. So while you might have preferred he consider only whether he could afford to make the loan, it wasn't unreasonable for him to take the reasons for your financial situation into account and comment on them.

Look, we know it's annoying to be taken to task, even if it's done with a lot more tact than your brother showed. But all you have to do to avoid that lecture in the future is not ask him for money.

My brother is trying to stiff us.

When someone doesn't repay a loan

Question: My wife and I lent $5,000 to my younger brother to buy a motorcycle. Jake signed a note saying the money was a loan and agreed to pay us $100 month, starting last January. It's now December, and he hasn't paid us a dime. Instead, whenever I ask about the money, he doesn't really answer. I'm pretty sure he's planning to stiff us, which is what he did to our dad a few years ago when he borrowed money for a car. Dad solved the problem by taking the car, selling it, and keeping the money. But Jake's my kid brother, and I don't want to do that. Is there something we can do to get our money back, or are we just stuck?

Answer: Having a close relative with a major moral flaw is a serious problem, and that's what you're facing. Your brother is a thief. Those may be harsh words, but what else do you call someone who walks off with your money and has no intention of returning it?

If you're unwilling to take the motorcycle from Jake or to hire a collection agency, your options are few and unappealing. Try to shame Jake into paying you back? He's proven his skin is too thick for that. Withhold something from him that he wants more than he wants to keep your money? Good luck finding a carrot sufficiently attractive. Forget about the loan? That may be all you can do, even though it means both losing your money *and* reinforcing your brother's bad behavior. Leading us to wonder: Are you sure you don't want to reconsider repossessing the bike?

Nobody's perfect, of course, and we all have relatives who forget birthdays, never say thank-you, or talk only about themselves. But these annoying people are not in a league with your brother. Relatives like Jake—people who lie, cheat, and steal—often become cancers in their families.

The real challenge you face is not how to retrieve your $5,000, but how, in the long run, to protect yourself and your family from your dishonest brother while finding a way to keep him in your heart.

ᕲ— HOW OTHERS DEAL WITH DEADBEATS —ᕲ

What do others do when faced with a deadbeat? Here's what the participants in our survey said when we asked them the following question:

"Suppose that two months ago a friend borrowed $100 from you and promised to pay you back last month. But they still haven't repaid you, and they've said nothing about the money. What would you be most likely to do?"

(continued)

PERCENT WHO ANSWERED

Nothing. I wouldn't care if I got my money back or not.	11%
Nothing. I don't like to confront people about things like this.	6%
Hint to them that I'd like my money back.	26%
Ask them for my money back.	57%

Source: Fleming & Schwarz survey.

Now you know why there are so many deadbeats. Forty-three percent of the people from whom they borrow money don't ask to be repaid. How much more encouragement do they need? As much as we hate to blame the victim, these too kind or too timid souls are a major reason why deadbeats get away with so much.

My brother won't let me repay a loan.

When a family member makes you feel like a poor relation

Question: Ten years ago, when my husband and I bought our home, my brother Marcus lent us $1,500 to help us furnish it. When I tried to pay him back a year later, Marcus wouldn't let me, saying the money had been a gift—a "house-warming present" he called it, even though he and his wife had given us an expensive fireplace set when we'd moved in.

Last year, when I needed to take some time off from

work to help my mother-in-law close down her home, I asked to borrow another $500, but only on the condition that it was a loan and not a gift. Marcus agreed. However, when I recently tried to repay him, Marcus refused to take my check and again insisted the money had been a gift.

While my husband and I appreciate Marcus's generosity, we also feel patronized. We're not as rich as Marcus, but we can afford to pay our bills, and we expect to repay the money we borrow. Shouldn't Marcus let us?

Answer: Yes, especially when you made a point of insisting that you be allowed to before accepting the $500. In recharacterizing the loans as gifts, Marcus was insensitive to your feelings, a lapse his kindness does not entirely excuse. More important, he seems not to understand—and perhaps does not want to understand—that you and your husband are self-reliant. You need to sit down with him and explain that as much as you appreciate his generosity, your self-respect demands that he allow you to repay the loans. Then hand him a check.

A friend I owe money to is pressuring me to help his girlfriend get a job.

What are your obligations when you're in someone's debt?

Question: Two months ago Spencer, a good friend from college who now makes lots of money on Wall Street, lent me $6,000, interest-free, so that I could pay off my credit cards, repay some debts, and generally get back on my feet financially. The loan has been a great help, and I am paying Spencer back at the rate of $250 a month. In the meantime, he has asked a big favor of me, namely: to arrange an "information interview" for his new girlfriend with an editor at the magazine where I recently got a job in the art department. While I've met a couple of the editors, I don't really know them (and vice versa), and I'd prefer not to ask for this sort of favor—something I wouldn't hesitate to tell Spencer if I didn't owe him so much money. Does accepting the loan obligate me to do this for him? I feel like he's taking advantage of the fact that I owe him money.

Answer: The great thing about borrowing money from a bank is that they write down everything they expect of you. Friends and family are a different story.

In the case at hand, you've put yourself in a position where Spencer is not wrong to expect a big favor from you, since that's exactly what you accepted from him. What he can't expect, however, is for you to compromise yourself. So, for example, had he asked you to be a reference for a woman you scarcely know, he'd be crossing that line. But asking you to play a chip with your boss is not unreasonable. After all, he's not requesting that you ask an editor to hire his girlfriend, just to talk to her. You owe your friend that favor, even if you'd prefer not to do it.

⌒ RISKY BUSINESS: LENDING BY THE NUMBERS ⌒

95 percent of adult Americans have lent money to friends or family members.

36 percent have made at least one loan greater than $1,000.

5 percent have made at least one loan greater than $20,000.

With respect to the largest loans people have made:

- 43 percent of the lenders were NOT repaid in full.

- 27 percent received NOTHING in the way of repayment.

- Size doesn't matter. Large loans and small loans were equally likely to not be repaid.

- About one out of three people with household incomes under $50,000 received nothing in repayment on the largest loan they ever made.

- About one out of five people with household incomes of $100,000 or more received nothing in repayment.

Source: *Money* survey.

The bottom line? Lending money to friends and relatives is a risky business. If you can't afford to not be repaid, be careful—very careful—in taking the measure of would-be borrowers.

Chapter Four

To Lend or Not to Lend

Acquaintance. A person whom we know well enough to borrow from, but not well enough to lend to.

—Ambrose Bierce

SOMETIMES ALL FRIENDS or relatives need from you is for you to feed the cat while they're away. Sometimes they need you to help move a couch or baby-sit for an hour. And sometimes what they need is money. Money to buy flowers for a girlfriend. Money to tide them over till payday. Money to buy a home or start a business. Money to pay for a wedding. Money to retain a divorce lawyer.

When you can easily afford to lend money to someone whom you love and who you know will repay you, the decision is a no-brainer. You happily write the check.

But what happens when the situation is not so cut-and-dried—when you're worried that you'll never see your money again unless you hound your brother-in-law for it, or when you know that your spendthrift daughter and her husband are going to burn through this loan, just like they did with the last one?

If unsettling thoughts like these don't keep you awake at night, there's always the other side of the coin to worry about: What happens if I *don't* lend them the money? Will the bank take their house? Will their children be computer-illiterate?

And then there are the nonfinancial ramifications of saying no: Will Christine stop talking to me? Would she go so far as to turn Brian against me, and, if so, does that mean he won't help fix my car?

Kidding aside, deciding whether to lend someone money often requires us to make an uncomfortable trade-off—a trade-off between our wallets and the people we care about. It's not a problem many of our parents prepared us to deal with. Maybe they occasionally voiced an opinion on the subject—something along the lines of "Your grandfather always said 'Where there's a loan, there's sure to be a fight,' " or "When it's family asking for help, you can never say no." Maybe they even argued about it once in a while ("I don't care if she is your sister, they never pay us back"). But unless we're from very unusual families, most of us find ourselves not at all sure about what to do the first time a friend or relative comes to us for a loan—or we go to them.

It's like flying without a compass. There's a whole lot of downside.

I lent money to my niece, and now her brother wants a loan.

Does lending money to one relative mean lending to all?

Question: My sister, who's divorced, has a twenty-three-year-old son and a twenty-one-year-old daughter, both of whom I'm very fond of. Recently, my niece—who just graduated from Howard and is working for the first time—asked to borrow $5,000 to help buy a car. She's a responsible, hard-working girl, and I said sure. Now her brother wants the same amount for the same reason. While he's a nice kid, he's always behind on his rent and is totally unreliable, and I don't want to lend him the money. Would it be unfair of me to refuse, given that I've helped out his sister?

Answer: Not at all. Your niece earned that loan. She has given you every reason to believe she could be trusted to use the money wisely and repay it on time, and there's nothing unfair about rewarding her good behavior.

But of course you're right to worry that your nephew might think you're playing favorites if you don't lend him $5,000 as well. To put that issue to rest, explain to him why you're unwilling to help out, and let him know that if he starts behaving more responsibly—say, if he goes for a year without having to ask for rent money—you'll reconsider.

More generally, you are under no obligation to lend money to one family member just because you lent some to another. And you certainly aren't required to suspend either

judgment or common sense in considering your relatives'—
or anyone else's—requests for help. Suppose your nephew
never matures (he wouldn't be the first). Unless he's facing
a clear emergency, you can keep your checkbook in the
drawer with a clear conscience. And that remains true no
matter how many loans you make to his sister.

⌒— SPLIT DOWN THE MIDDLE —⌒

Fifty percent of the public believe you should never lend
money to a relative. The other fifty percent disagree.
Source: *Money* survey.

The older you are, the more likely you are to think lending
money to relatives is a bad idea. For example, 64 percent of
people over the age of fifty-five think you shouldn't do it,
while only 38 percent of people under the age of thirty-five
think it's a mistake.

Are older people wiser, or just more cynical? We'd say
both.

Her boyfriend's moving to Europe, and my friend wants a loan so she can pursue him.

When a friend wants money for something foolish

Question: A good friend who recently left her husband has
met a new guy, and unfortunately he's about to move to
Brussels. Leah's plan is to follow him to Belgium, even

though he hasn't encouraged her. She's sure that they're soul mates and that he'll realize this if they spend more time together.

Because her money's tied up by the divorce, Leah's asked me to lend her several thousand dollars, which I can afford and which I know she'll pay back. However, I think this is a very foolish thing for Leah to do and she'll wind up regretting it. Is it okay to refuse to lend her the money?

Answer: If Leah wanted the money to support a heroin habit or to hire a hit man to take out her soon-to-be-ex-husband, you'd be right to say no. But what Leah plans to do is, it would seem, merely foolish. Moreover, she's an adult, and adults get to make their own mistakes. So ethically speaking, there's no compelling reason for you to refuse her the money.

By the same token, there's also no compelling reason for you to make the loan. This isn't an emergency. And from what you've said about Leah, she could probably get the money elsewhere. So to answer your question: It's your money, and you don't have to lend it to her to do something you think is wrongheaded.

Still, we think you should reconsider. It's not that we're any more sanguine than you are about the chances of Leah finding true love pursuing a man who's content to leave her behind. It's because you're Leah's friend, not her guardian. And what are friends for if not to accept us as who we are, even if who we are is sometimes a bit imprudent?

∽— **WHAT DO YOU NEED MY MONEY FOR, ANYHOW?** —∾

According to the Federal Reserve, this is what people say they do with the money they borrow from their friends and relatives:

Buy things they need or want	30%
Take care of an emergency	25%
Fund a small business	15%
Go to school	12%
Buy a home	9%
Other	9%

Source: *Money*/Federal Reserve Survey of Consumer Finances.

Is it up to me to keep my nephew out of jail?

When your spendthrift sister needs help you don't want to give

Question: My sister Ally's boy was a decent kid until he got to high school, but now Justin's always getting into trouble. Recently he and his friends stole a car, and as a result he may end up in a juvenile detention facility. Ally says she's found a very good lawyer who thinks he can keep Justin from being locked up. But Ally can't afford the lawyer, so she's asked me to lend her $7,500.

I want to help my sister and my nephew, but here's the problem: The only reason Ally and her husband can't afford a lawyer is that they spend every cent they make and then some. New cars, new clothes, new electronic gear. You name it, they've got it all. Just last year they remodeled their kitchen for the second time in eight years.

I know if I lend Ally the money she'll repay me, but it will take a while. In the meantime, my wife and I will have to postpone the work we've been planning to do on our home. I realize that keeping my nephew out of what amounts to jail is a lot more important than replacing our carpets and refinishing our floors. But I don't see why this should fall on me when my sister and her husband make good money and just throw it away. What should I do?

Answer: Order the carpeting and schedule the floor guy.

If your sister owns a home (and you say she does), somewhere there's a financial institution that will lend her $7,500 against it. Given their spendthrift ways, she and her husband may have already borrowed quite a bit against the house, and, if that's the case, the cost of another loan will be high. If it's too high, they can get a cash advance on their credit cards or sell a car. But whatever it costs them to raise the $7,500, that's their problem, not yours.

It's not as if your sister has fallen ill and can't afford to care for her family. On the contrary, this is a case of a husband and wife failing to care for their family—failing in the sense that their self-indulgent spending came at the expense of what every family needs: some money socked away for a rainy day. You and your wife are under no obligation to make sacrifices to reduce the cost to your sister of her spendthrift ways.

I don't want to be my brother's bank.

When you don't want to start lending someone money because you fear it will never stop

Question: Over the years, my older brother has asked me for a loan three or four times. Tony's a hardworking guy, but he's not much of a saver or planner. I've always said no, not because I couldn't afford it, but because I can see the handwriting on the wall. Though I'm not rich and he's not poor, I fear that Tony is the type of guy who'd think that if I had the money to lend him, I must not really need it, and so he'd never get around to repaying me. I'm starting to worry, though, that instead of being smart, I've just been a piker. Recently Tony's asked me to lend him $500. Should I do it?

Answer: Persistent devil, your brother.

Your reasons for being reluctant to lend him money are understandable. They'd be more persuasive, though, if you'd lent him money, and he'd either failed to repay it, only repaid it at your insistence, or started hitting you up for more all the time.

Instead, what you've been doing is practicing a kind of preventive tough love. While Tony hasn't actually done anything wrong, you've refused to let him get into a position where he can. What you haven't been practicing is generosity and kindness.

So give Tony the benefit of the doubt, and lend him the money. Unless he has, say, stiffed other relatives in the past or had perennial credit problems, he's your brother, and he deserves a chance to prove your instincts wrong. Of course, if he fails to do so, you'll have an excellent reason for saying no in the future.

⌒— SERIAL BORROWERS —⌒

Is the author of the previous letter a little paranoid? Or does he have good reason to worry that a brother who borrows from him once is likely to want to revisit the well?

We asked the participants in our survey whether they agreed or disagreed that "In most families, there's somebody who's always trying to borrow money from everyone else."

Here are their responses:

PERCENT WHO

Strongly agree	22%
Somewhat agree	37%
Somewhat disagree	33%
Strongly disagree	8%

Source: Fleming & Schwarz survey.

What does this mean? Most people know their family has a serial borrower in its midst, another third are slow to admit it, and a very small percent of the population has gotten off lucky.

Must we throw our money away?

When an irresponsible friend needs help

Question: Good friends who've fallen behind in their mortgage payments and are in danger of losing their home have asked to borrow a large sum of money. My wife and I can afford to lend it to them. But between their habit of always spending twice as much as they make and the fact that they're living in a place they couldn't afford even if they were prudent, they'll never be able to pay us back. Our problem: These friends have been very generous to us in the past, treating us to nice dinners, taking us to concerts and shows, and impulsively buying us expensive gifts. Does this obligate us to say yes to a loan we're sure amounts to throwing money down a rat hole?

Answer: Well, you're certainly under no obligation to throw more money down that rat hole than you can afford to lose. But that said, get out your checkbook. Rat hole or no, you're obligated to lend money to the people from whom you've accepted so much—and whose financial demise you contributed to by allowing them to pick up the tab for those lavish meals and pricey tickets. Since you were part of the problem, you need to try to be part of the solution.

We hope you get your money back. But we realize for that to happen, your friends would probably have to have personality transplants.

ᦉ— FRIENDS NO MORE —ᦉ

Eight out of ten people believe that lending money to
someone is a good way to ruin a friendship.

Source: Fleming & Schwarz survey.

To Lend or Not to Lend
A FEW RULES OF THUMB

So someone asks if you can lend him some money. Maybe
you're sure the right answer is yes, or maybe you're sure it's
no. Fine. But what if you're uncertain about how to respond? If that's the case, try considering each of the following points:

1. How serious the borrower's need for the money is—not
   just in his or her mind, but from your perspective as
   well—and the reasons why the borrower can't pay for
   what he or she needs without help.

2. How close you are to the borrower.

3. Whether the borrower has ever lent money to you or your
   family, or otherwise been generous to you.

4. The degree to which you would like to see the borrower
   have whatever the money is for.

5. The size of the loan.

6. The likelihood that the loan will be repaid. This means taking into account both the character of the borrower—namely, how obligated he or she will feel to pay you back—and the odds that he or she simply won't be able to pay you back.

7. The economic implications for you if the borrower should either fail to repay you or be slow to repay you.

8. What other options are open for the borrower if you say no.

Unfortunately there's no magic formula that tells you how to make trade-offs between the issues these points raise. But that doesn't mean that being analytic is a waste of time. Whether your nephew wants to borrow $2,500 to buy the clothes and equipment he needs to become a rodeo cowboy or $25,000 to buy out the owner of the bike shop he's been managing for the past three years, it makes sense to consider the likelihood of his succeeding and the likelihood of his walking away from the debt if he fails.

While ethics obligates us to try to help our friends and family, it doesn't require us to say yes every time one of them asks for a loan. On the contrary, it's perfectly reasonable to say no if:

1. You can't afford to lend the money.

2. The real reason the would-be borrower needs money is because of his own extravagant ways.

3. There's a reasonably good chance that the person who wants to borrow the money may not pay it back, and you can't afford to have the loan turn into a gift.

4. You have no interest in helping the would-be borrower with the problem the money is intended to solve, for example: You disapprove of what the borrower plans to do with the money, or you don't feel the borrower's problem should be your problem.

What doesn't wash, however, is to always find a reason to say no. As Benjamin Franklin might have had Poor Richard say: Analysis is not the enemy of generosity. Instead it should be generosity's companion.

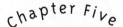

Chapter Five

That's Not How I Remember It

---- ⟨⟨⟨⟩⟩⟩ ----

Always leave a little room for a mistake.

—Chinese proverb

HAVE YOU HEARD this one?: A guy with a duck on his head walks into a psychiatrist's office, and the psychiatrist says, "So how can I help?" To which the duck answers, "Well to start with, you can get this guy off my ass."

Like many jokes, this one is built on misunderstanding and surprise: Things are not as they seem.

Unfortunately, when misunderstanding and surprise find their way into the area where money, ethics, and personal relationships intersect, rarely is there much to laugh about.

∾

I'm sure the loan is due, but my brother says it isn't.

When the borrower and lender disagree
on the terms of the agreement

Question: My brother borrowed $30,000 from me a couple of years ago to help pay for his wife's infertility treatments. The good news is they're now the parents of triplets. The bad news is my brother's convinced he doesn't have to start repaying me for another two years, when in fact he's supposed to start paying me now. We never put anything in writing, but I'm sure I'm right because I remember thinking the payments would start the same year I turned forty. My wife and I have plenty of expenses of our own, and I'd really like to start getting my money back. How can I make my brother realize that this is what we agreed to?

Answer: You can't. Without either a written document expressing the terms of your agreement, or a witness to your oral agreement whose memory and honesty you both trust completely, it's just your word—and memory—against his.

So how can the two of you resolve this disagreement? You could flip a coin—or arm wrestle, if you prefer—with the winner to decide when the repayment is to start. Or you could split the difference with your brother—that is, he could begin paying you back not now (the date you recall) and not in two years (his date), but in one year.

We know, we know. You're sure you're right about what

the deal was, and unless you win the coin toss, these solutions aren't fair to you. But that's what happens when you don't write things down: Misunderstandings arise, and compromise replaces justice.

◦— PRESUMED ACCURATE —◦

Nobody's memory is perfect, of course. But, when it comes to borrowing and lending, do some people remember the deal better than others?

To shed some light on this issue, we asked the participants in our survey: "If you heard about a dispute in which a person says their friend owes them $250 and the friend says they owe the person $150, whom would you be most likely to believe: the lender or the borrower?"

Here are their responses:

PERCENT WHO SAY

The lender, who says their friend owes them $250.	73%
The borrower, who says they owe the person $150.	27%

Source: Fleming & Schwarz survey.

Ask this question of folks age thirty and older, and they are significantly more likely than younger adults to side with the lender. To us, this suggests that people in their twenties are still learning the truth of Benjamin Franklin's observation that we noted earlier: Creditors have better memories than debtors.

Was it a gift or was it a loan?

When your mother wants her money back

Question: Ten years ago, when I was starting my landscaping business, my mother gave me $12,000. I signed a note saying I borrowed the money, but that's all. There was no interest, and no mention of when the loan was due. I always believed the money was really a gift, and the only reason Mom wanted the note was in case she fell on hard times. Now, however, my mother wants me to start paying her back, even though she's doing fine financially. I suspect my tightfisted stepfather is behind this. Am I right to feel Mom's betrayed me?

Answer: Disappointed, sure. But betrayed? Probably not.

What's clear is this: If your mother had intended the $12,000 to be a gift, she wouldn't have asked you to sign that note. So unless she explicitly assured you that the note was meaningless, your mother's done nothing wrong. No one is obligated to keep a promise they didn't make.

It would be nice, though, if your mother offered you an explanation. Having called the note after a decade of silence, she should, as a matter of courtesy, tell you her reason for now wanting the money.

P.S. As unpleasant as you may find the position you're in, look on the bright side: Although it turns out your mother didn't give you $12,000, she did give you a large, interest-free loan for ten years. That's a pretty nice gift in itself.

My uncles claim my Dad owed them money.

When someone asks you to repay your father's debt

Question: After my eighty-four-year-old father died, his two brothers told me they'd each lent him $1,000 to help pay his property taxes a couple of years ago. There's enough in Dad's estate to repay them, and I have no reason to believe my uncles are dishonest. But I was close to my father, and he never said anything to me about these loans. There's nothing in writing, by the way, not even a canceled check (my uncles say they gave him cash). Should I give them the money, or what?

Answer: We understand why you might doubt your uncles. Still, you're obligated to take their claims seriously, even though you're not obligated to assume that they're legitimate. This means, for example, reviewing your father's bank accounts to see if there were cash deposits around the time his property taxes were due. And it means discreetly asking others in your family whether they ever heard of these loans or whether they were approached for money themselves.

Unless your research convinces you that there was no debt, we suggest you pay your uncles. It's not that we think you should reward dishonorable behavior—or confusion—if that's what's going on. But if there's any chance your dad borrowed the money, it's important that his debts be repaid.

Should you conclude, however, that your father's estate

owes your uncles nothing, be forewarned: This is the kind of thing families take sides over. So even if you believe your uncles are a couple of octogenarian reprobates who are lying through their dental implants, ask yourself whether you want to start a family feud over $2,000.

⌒— SO MUCH FOR A HANDSHAKE —⌒

Imagine yourself in a position not unlike the position of the writer of the last letter. Specifically, your elderly father recently died, and now one of his old friends tells you that your dad owed him several thousand dollars. This is the first time you've ever heard of the loan, and the friend says he has no documentation for it. He says that he and your dad always did things on a handshake.

In this situation, would you be most likely to:

- Pay your father's friend the money.
- Pay your father's friend something, but not the whole amount.
- Not pay your father's friend.
- Call the police—this is a scam.

That's the question we put to survey participants, and here are their answers:

(continued)

PERCENT WHO SAY

Pay your father's friend the money.	6%
Pay something, but not the whole amount.	13%
Not pay your father's friend.	70%
Call the police—this is a scam.	11%

Source: Fleming & Schwarz survey.

Most people have reservations about the legitimacy of agreements that haven't been written down. Here you see just how powerful those reservations are.

What you also see, of course, is just how strong the impulse is to hang on to our money.

My father-in-law's making money on his loan to us.

When your spouse's family sees things differently than yours does

Question: Is it right to charge interest on a loan to a close family member? My husband's father recently lent my husband and me a large amount of money so that we could open our first restaurant. We've agreed to pay him interest at the same rate he'd be earning if he'd left his money in his money market account. My husband and I have been satisfied with the arrangement. But my brother says my father-in-law is not being very generous, and that he shouldn't be making money off of us.

Answer: Not only are your brother's analytic skills lacking, but he's a troublemaker to boot. Your father-in-law is doing you and your husband a big favor. As you must know, most new restaurants fail, hence banks rarely make commercial loans to restaurants—especially to first-time restaurateurs. Without your father-in-law, you would probably have had to borrow against your house to raise the money, and—if you did—you'd be paying a much higher interest rate than he's charging you.

So the benefits to you and your husband of your father-in-law's loan are considerable: You have the money you need. Your home is not encumbered by additional debt. And the cost to you is much lower than the cost of a second mortgage (interest on a second mortgage is generally two to three times higher than the interest paid by money market funds, plus mortgage lenders charge points on the loan).

As a family member, was your father-in-law obligated to be even more generous and to not charge interest at all? In a word, no—not any more than he was obligated to make the money a gift. It's true that in some families relatives never charge each other interest. But in many other families they do, and neither practice is more ethical than the other.

Our advice: Tell your brother to calm down. Your husband's dad is doing you a good turn for which you have every reason to be appreciative.

↶— NOT IN MY FAMILY, WE DON'T. —↷

Two out of three people believe you should never charge interest on a loan to a relative.

Source: *Money* survey.

My father thinks I don't trust him.

When your parents refuse to put the loan in writing

Question: My parents, who own a home near Cleveland, would like to buy a condominium in Florida. Their idea is to spend winters in the condo and someday move there permanently. To help with the purchase, they've asked me to lend them $18,000. I said I would. But when I asked my folks to sign a note acknowledging the loan, my father became indignant and said he wasn't about to sign anything. He said that his word is his bond and that I should trust him. I do trust him, but here's the problem: His health isn't great, and he's almost sure to die before Mom. Since Mom pays no attention to financial matters, my sister Donna—with whom I don't get along—is bound to end up taking care of things for her. And Donna's the last person in the world I'd want to bring up an undocumented loan to. What should I do?

Answer: Hope that Donna dies first. . . . Sorry, we couldn't resist.

Obviously, memorializing a loan in writing is the best way to avoid future misunderstandings, and your father is being naive—and very unfair to you—in refusing to do so. Even so, you don't necessarily want to deny your folks the loan just because your father is being pigheaded. Hence we encourage you to consult a lawyer, who can tell you (1) how a loan can be documented other than with a written agreement (it can be done) and (2) the likelihood of your collecting should things get ugly with your sister.

We realize that "things getting ugly with your sister" is exactly what you'd like to avoid. Still, we hope you'll investigate your options and see if there isn't some way for you to accomplish the good deed your father is making it so difficult for you to perform.

Get It in Writing

"Why do I need to get it in writing? I wouldn't lend him the money if I didn't trust him."

"Put it on paper? Why should I? He knows I'm good for it."

"Why would we bother writing this up? Neither of us is going to forget."

Nice sentiments, but wrong answers.

Here's why you should document every lending arrangement in which you are involved: to preserve your relationships with your friends and family and to preserve your money as well.

Do we mean even a loan of twenty or thirty bucks? Not really. But any time you lend an amount it would hurt not to have repaid, you should put the loan in writing.

To begin with, no one's memory is perfect. Sure, most people are unlikely to forget a $1,000 loan. But when the lender distinctly remembers the borrower saying "I'll pay you back by the end of the year" and the borrower distinctly remembers telling the lender "I'll pay you back as soon as I can," the friendship is about to be tested.

Imperfect memories aren't the only reason undocumented loans lead to trouble. As the writer of the last letter pointed out, people can die before they repay a loan, creating another whole set of problems. Imagine having to tell the widow of a friend who died unexpectedly that her just-deceased husband owed you money.

Finally, there's the chiseler problem, to wit: Unwritten agreements provide dishonest people with the opportunity to play games. You may know damn well that your brother-in-law understands he's supposed to repay you at the rate of $300 a month. But if he says you agreed to $200 a month, you can't very well call your sister's husband a liar.

It's not as if writing down a loan is a cumbersome process. All it involves is specifying three things, generally in no more than a sentence or two. The three things are:

1. The amount of the money being borrowed.

2. The date or dates the money is to be repaid.

3. The rate of interest.

If the loan is interest-free, say so. It's silence on this point that leads to misunderstandings, at best, and feelings of resentment, at worst.

If the date(s) on which the loan is to be repaid can't be determined, be as specific as possible (e.g., "The loan is to be repaid when John and Emily receive the money from the sale of their current home," "The loan is to be repaid no later than five years from the date of this agreement").

If the lender is content to let the borrower keep the money indefinitely provided the lender doesn't need it back, that should be written down. It's capturing the expectations of both parties that is critically important. And a great virtue of having to write them down is that it flushes out these expectations, often preventing future misunderstandings.

There is no reason for a loan agreement to be either long or legalistic. Here are two examples of the kind of short document that will minimize the misunderstandings that can arise when friends and relatives lend money to one another:

Jack Burns and Tom Meehan hereby acknowledge that, on December 1, 2007, Jack borrowed $2,500 from Tom, and that Jack will repay the loan on December 1, 2008, with 6 percent interest.

Chandra Williams and Eva Carmichael hereby acknowledge that, on November 1, 2007, Eva borrowed $1,500 from Chandra and that Eva will repay Chandra at the rate of $150 per month beginning on the first of March, 2008, and continuing monthly through the first of December, 2008. There is no interest on this loan.

Would a lawyer write these documents differently? Of course. Our concern is not preparing for a legal dispute (though these examples would look pretty good in court). Our concern is preventing important relationships from being undermined by a misunderstanding or by someone's less-than-perfect memory. That's why an absence of ambiguity and the inclusion of the amount, interest rate, and due date(s) are so critical.

Two other things are critical as well.

1. Every person mentioned in the note should sign it.

2. Every person should get a signed copy.

There's one final thing you should document in writing, and that's the repayment of the note. All this requires is that the lender write "paid in full" on the note and sign and date it. In a perfect world, all involved would then toss their copies of the note into their important papers drawer. But the world being less than perfect and people's memories being less than perfect as well, the borrower is well advised to hang on to the note lest the lender forget that the loan was repaid.

What's wrong with a canceled check? Nothing. Copy it and put it with the note. But a check alone won't do you much good if a loving but confused aunt or an absent-minded in-law insists "That must have been for something else. I'd remember if you'd paid me."

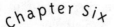

chapter six

Rich Brother, Poor Brother

―――――――――――― ⟨⟨⟨⟨⟩ ――――――――――――

Brothers love each other when they are equally rich.
—African proverb

IF YOU HAVE a lot more—or a lot less—money, education, or social status than your brother or sister, join the club. It's a big one.

According to sociologist Dalton Conley, children who grow up in the same home frequently wind up with very different incomes as adults. Specifically, he says that in America "over half of all [economic] inequality is *within* families, not *between* them." In other words, wealth and income gaps between brothers and sisters from the same family are more common than wealth and income gaps between different families.

How can we have the same parents, spend our childhoods together, and still find ourselves in such different financial circumstances as adults?

Part of the answer, of course, is that just because we're related doesn't mean we're all equally ambitious, talented, or smart—or that we care about the same things. After all, some folks are bitten by the acting bug, and others are bitten by the captain-of-industry bug.

Another part of the answer, though, may surprise you: According to Conley, often only nominally do we grow up in the same families and the same environments. One daughter may grow up having to work after school because Dad is struggling to get his business started. Yet by the time her younger sister reaches high school, Dad's business may be prospering and little sister's after-school life may include tutors who are helping her get into the best college possible. Or one son may grow up with the financial and emotional security provided by a sound marriage, while his younger brother may have to live with the economic setbacks and emotional turmoil that occur when their parents divorce. Or one brother may graduate from college as the economy is going into a recession, take a data-processing job at a hospital, and live modestly forever after. But three years later, just as the economy begins roaring back to health, his younger brother may graduate from college, get a job on Wall Street, and live prosperously forever after.

In short, Conley says there are three factors that often lead to substantial disparities in the incomes of brothers and sisters. One is large social forces that change over time—the state of the economy, for example. The second is family-specific events, such as a divorce or a layoff. And the third factor is this: Parents treat their children differently when they raise them. In particular, for good reasons and bad, parents often invest more money and time in some of their children than in others.

Regardless of their origins, wealth gaps between siblings—and wealth gaps between other family members as well—give rise to any number of difficult situations. The following pages consider a few of the thornier ones.

$\sim$

I just made a million bucks, and I don't want my brothers to know.

Must you tell your family you're rich?

Question: When the small high-tech company I work for was acquired recently, my stock options were suddenly worth over $1,000,000. Is it okay to say nothing about this to my brothers? They have good jobs, but neither has this kind of money. I'm worried they'll think of me differently if they find out about my new wealth. I'm also concerned that, since they tend to be extravagant guys, they'll turn to me for a loan every time they want a new car or even the latest mountain bike.

Answer: Do you think your brothers tell you all *their* secrets?

There's nothing unethical about keeping your financial status private. The truth is, it's not obligatory—or even necessarily desirable—to tell everything to everyone, including family. Indeed, the idea that honesty requires us to keep nothing to ourselves mistakes prudence for a lack of integrity. While your brothers might very well be interested in knowing your net worth, they have no right to know it.

So there's no need to feel guilty if you choose to keep your big score to yourself. Be forewarned, however, that money has a way of making its presence known. Take a trip to Paris when you usually vacation in the Poconos, or buy a new Lexus to replace your old Hyundai, and your relatives are going to get the picture. So rather than relying on discretion alone, follow the sage advice Charles Barkley gave LeBron James when James signed his big NBA contract: Learn to say no.

⌒— DON'T TELL, DON'T ASK —⌒

Eight out of ten people say you should never let your relatives know how much money you have.

Source: *Money* survey.

Why should my sister's child get all the goodies?

When some cousins have a lot more than others

Question: My sister Anna and I were very close growing up, and we've remained close as adults (we even teach at the same school). We each have a twelve-year-old son— our only children—and we'd like them to be as close as we are. But here's the problem: Anna's husband makes a lot more than my husband does, and we can't afford the things they give their child. For example, while they often take our son Zach with them on family ski trips, their son Daniel always has the latest equipment, while Zach gets his old gear.

Now Anna tells me they plan to send Daniel to a private school in the fall—something we can't possibly afford— and I'm worried this will lead to a great divide between the boys. I also think it's unfair—unfair that one cousin should have so much more than the other for no reason except that the man one sister married makes much more money than the man the other sister married. What do you think?

Answer: The unfairness you cite—the privileges your nephew enjoys and the distance those privileges inevitably create between him and your son—is rooted in an inescapable fact of life, namely: Money matters. When we think about our relationships with loved ones we don't want it to matter. We may even feel that it shouldn't matter. But it does.

You can't expect your sister to deny her son the best education possible in order to ensure that he remains close to Zach. Nor can you expect her and her husband to supply Zach with all the things they deliver to their own son.

Not that you suggested they should. We mention this only to make the point that no one has done anything wrong here. No one has behaved unethically, and no one has treated anyone unfairly. To us, it sounds as if your sister and her husband have been both kind and considerate to your son. You can't ask for more than that.

⇘— **NOT THAT WE GET TO CHOOSE, BUT . . .** —⇙

Three out of four people say they would rather have a rich brother than a poor brother.

Source: Fleming & Schwarz survey.

My in-laws-to-be live in a trailer park,
and I'm starting to worry.

When you marry into a very poor family

Question: My fiancée, Lee Ann, is a librarian, and I'm an engineer. We recently went to Kentucky, where she grew up, so I could meet her family. I knew they didn't have a lot, but still I was surprised to find that her parents, her sister, and her sister's three children live in a run-down trailer park. The only way to describe them is that they're terribly poor and completely uneducated. So now I'm wondering: What will my financial obligation to these folks be when Lee Ann and I are married?

Answer: True love is a wonderful thing. But poverty isn't, and you're not wrong to be concerned about the ramifications of marrying into a family as lacking in financial resources as Lee Ann's.

Once the vows are spoken, you'll have an obligation to come to your in-laws' aid. After all, they'll be family. While having more money than they do doesn't obligate you to do for them everything you and Lee Ann will be doing for yourselves (you don't have to, say, buy them a house or car), you certainly have to help them in an emergency. And if Lee Ann's family is as poor as you say, just about any bump in the road—the clutch giving out or the rent going up—could become an emergency.

We suggest you talk to Lee Ann about what she expects the two of you as a couple will do for her family. In the process, you might ask her what she's currently doing for them. For example: Does she send her folks money on a regular basis, and if so, how much and how often? What does she consider an emergency, and how does she usually respond? And, more fundamentally, is Lee Ann someone who never says no to her family's requests?

We wish you luck in working this out. And as you do, you might keep this in mind: There are undoubtedly a few things about your family that are giving Lee Ann pause as well.

✆— THE RICH MAN, POOR MAN BLUES —✆

Fifty-five percent of the public say they have run into trouble as a result of having a lot *more* money than a friend or relative.

and

Fifty-seven percent say they have run into trouble as a result of having a lot *less* money than a friend or relative.

Source: *Money* survey.

Whichever side of the fence you're on, it isn't easy.

My brothers can't stand to hear me talk about my life.

When a rich relative's wealth grates

Question: I'm a lawyer, and I travel a lot on business. After a recent family party, my two brothers took me aside and said that they were sick of me "showing off" in front of their kids and making them "look like losers." Specifically, they want me to stop mentioning my business trips to Asia, our family vacations, and the work my wife and I are doing on our house. But here's what gets me. They talk about the exact same stuff themselves—their work, their homes, and their vacations. Could they possibly be right that, because I'm more successful than they are, I'm obligated to never refer to the way my family and I live? I should add that these guys live comfortably. Paul and his wife own and operate a temp agency, and Kevin is a manager with the water district.

Answer: If you've been bragging—or simply dominating family gatherings with talk of yourself—they were right to object, and you should stop. But when your brothers accuse you of making them look like losers, it sounds to us as if you've struck a different nerve.

The problem is not that you've violated some code of ethics you didn't know about (you haven't). It is, we suspect, that you've lost sight of a law of human nature, namely that remarks which constitute casual, friendly conversation with your economic peers can play as showing off to folks who have less money—especially when they're relatives. You say you have to leave early because you're flying to a meeting in Tokyo the next day. But what your brothers hear is "I'm a really important guy who meets with people who wouldn't give you the time of day." You say the contractor who's installing the granite slabs in your new kitchen is driving you crazy, and they hear "We buy really expensive stuff—stuff you couldn't afford." And so on.

Look at it this way: If one of your brothers worked in an emergency room, would you want to spend Thanksgiving dinner hearing about accidents and illnesses? Well, hearing about all the money you spend and the people you rub shoulders with apparently is as unsettling to them as hospital horror stories might be to you.

That said, unless you really have been bragging, Paul and Kevin have overreacted in so sternly taking you to task. Not that we suggest you tell them that. Practically speaking, your best bet for ensuring harmony is to bow to their sensitivities and limit the number of stories you tell that include details that reflect your prosperity.

ᅌ— WHO'S THE BOSS? —ᅌ

Does having more money than your brothers and sisters put you in charge of your family? To find out what most people think, we asked the participants in our survey whether they agreed or disagreed with the following two statements:

- In most families, the adult child with the most money generally thinks they should be in charge of major family decisions.

(continued)

• In most families, the adult child with the most money generally *is* in charge of major family decisions.

Here are their responses:

	PERCENT WHO AGREE	PERCENT WHO DISAGREE
Richest think they should be in charge.	58%	42%
Richest are in charge.	57%	43%

Source: Fleming & Schwarz survey.

So there you have it. A solid majority believe that the richest sibling both expects to be and is the boss.

This doesn't mean, though, that the other brothers and sisters believe their richer sibling is entitled to that role. Indeed, it's not difficult to imagine a situation in which a rich brother wants and expects to be the boss, while his less prosperous siblings are muttering, "Who put him in charge?"

My sister is making a bundle, but she's a tightwad with me.

When a relative hits the jackpot

Question: I make a good living as an insurance agent, but my sister Amy, who works on Wall Street, makes a whole lot more. For the past few years, Amy and her husband and my wife and I have rented a condo in the Caribbean over the holidays. The condo belongs to someone Amy knows, so she always pays for it, then I give her half the rent while we're there. Last year, shortly before we left, I read in the paper that Amy's firm had had an exceptionally good year and that people like Amy would be getting seven-figure bonuses. So I was a little disappointed when she still asked me for the rent. I would have thought that, with a million-dollar check coming her way, Amy might at least have treated us to the condo. What do you think?

Answer: We think it reflects well on Amy that she didn't patronize you by insisting on picking up your share of a tab you can well afford to pay. You make a good living. Do you really want to be her poor relation, always hoping for a free ride?

Which isn't to say that Amy shouldn't be generous with you and your wife. She should, just as you should share some of your good fortune with your less successful friends and relatives. Still, when you go out with folks who make less than you do but who aren't what anyone would call poor, do you feel obligated to pick up the check? Okay then, why should Amy?

Distracted as you understandably are by your sister's big payday, you seem to have lost sight of what we're certain you know, namely: Making more money than the person you're with doesn't mean that you should be treating them to the things you routinely do together—not when they can well afford to pay their own way.

My sister got the prime cuts and I got the leftovers.

When one of you got all the breaks and the other got none

Question: My older sister Melissa and I grew up in a well-to-do family. But when I was in my teens, my father lost everything through a series of bad investments. As a result, my parents had to take me out of private school and were unable to send me to college. I struggled as a young adult, but ultimately I got a degree in computer programming, then saved enough to make the down payment on a small house.

Melissa, on the other hand, was never affected by our parents' misfortune. She grew up in a world of affluence, and by the time Dad went broke, she had already graduated from USC, where she'd met her future husband, a stockbroker who makes boatloads of money. Now all Melissa worries about is which $500 designer handbag to buy.

Since Melissa's been blessed with good luck all her life, shouldn't she feel some sense of obligation to help me out? I know I'd feel guilty if I were her, but all she does is criticize me for not accomplishing more.

Answer: Of course you're right that your sister, on whom fortune seems to have smiled, should be generous with you. If she hasn't helped you when you needed it and she could afford to, shame on her. And shame on her as well if she's been dismissive of what you've achieved by dint of your own hard work.

But here's the thing. What your sister is *not* obligated to do is make it up to you that your privileged childhood ended prematurely while hers didn't. Neither did marrying a man who can afford her taste in handbags place her in your debt. If you'd been forced to make sacrifices so Melissa could remain in college, that would be one thing. But none of Melissa's good fortune came at your expense, as tempting as it may be for you to see it that way. Consequently, her obligation to you is that of any sister to another: to be kind, to be loving, and to try to be helpful.

⌒ RICH BROTHER, POOR BROTHER—IT'S A BIG CLUB ⌒

- One out of four of us has a brother or sister who has a job that is much more—or much less—prestigious than our own (for example, one sibling is a lawyer and the other is a laborer).

- If you graduated from a four-year college (and are not an only child), the odds are one out of two that you have a brother or sister who didn't.

- Differences in accumulated wealth between siblings account for *90 percent* of all differences in wealth between individuals. In other words, if your brother's or sister's net worth is a lot lower or higher than yours, you're normal.

Source: Dalton Conley, *The Pecking Order*, Vintage Books: 2004.

I'm worried that my father-in-law is spending too much on us.

When someone with less money gives you an expensive gift

Question: My father-in-law gives each of his children, as well as their spouses, a nice check for their birthdays. My husband and I have significantly more money than his father—we own a chain of dry cleaners, he's a retired building super living on Social Security—so I feel uncomfortable accepting these checks. My husband doesn't think it's a problem, but I'd like to ask my father-in-law to stop. Do you agree that this would be the right thing to do?

Answer: Unless this is money your father-in-law truly can't afford to part with—unless passing out those checks is literally taking food off his table—the answer is no.

Gift-giving is an important social act for adults. It is a way of expressing love, appreciation, and good wishes. It is also a way of expressing self-respect, connectedness to family, and good cheer on celebratory occasions. And finally, gift-giving is an expression of one's role in the family—in your father-in-law's case, as paterfamilias.

Your good intentions notwithstanding, the idea that gifts should only flow from those with more money to those with less is patronizing. After all, how would you feel if a well-heeled friend returned your nice holiday gift with words to the effect that "You need this more than I do"?

Your father-in-law can hardly be unaware of the gap between your wealth and his, and it's to his credit that he doesn't use it as an excuse to forgo gift-giving.

Which isn't to say that spending more than you can afford on a gift is either smart or emblematic of virtue. But even if your father-in-law is writing checks that are a bit bigger than they should be, you and your husband have the opportunity to be generous to him as well, and to, in effect, make up any shortfall his gifts to you may be causing.

So relax. Accept your father-in-law's checks with the gratitude and warmth they deserve. Then treat yourself to something nice with the money, and tell him how much you enjoyed it.

My son the architect versus my son the actor

When it comes to family, should the professionals support the artists?

Question: I have two sons, Tyler and Jeremy. Tyler, who graduated from Brown three years ago, is a talented actor trying to make it in New York. Jeremy, who's about to start a graduate program in architecture, is a savvy, ambitious guy who I'm sure will have a very successful career. Recently, Tyler told me he realized that, even though he was the "big brother" in the family, he'd probably end up looking to Jeremy for help, instead of the other way around, since most actors are poor. The problem is, Jeremy's a bit of a tightwad. What can I do to encourage my younger son to realize he needs to help Tyler?

Answer: You're asking the wrong question. You should be asking what you can do to encourage Tyler to take responsibility for his financial future, rather than bolstering his belief that he can rely on handouts from his brother.

It's not that we think you're wrong to want Jeremy to be generous. But Tyler is making important decisions about his life right now, decisions that will play a critical role in determining how much money he has in the future. One of the things he needs to realize is that life involves making trade-offs, and that if he is going to pursue a career such as acting, he may well live less comfortably than if he chose a different career. In particular, Tyler shouldn't be encouraged to think that there *are* no trade-offs because brother Jeremy will make up the difference for him. Neither should he imagine that, as a would-be actor, he is exempt from the ethical obligation we all have to provide for ourselves.

And there's one more thing to consider. In order to have that successful career you envision him having, Jeremy is going to have to work very hard. Generally the people willing to do that are not indifferent to money. In fact, they typically have plans of their own for the money they earn, and the plans of even the most generous among them rarely include perpetually passing out big chunks of cash to healthy, intelligent, well-educated siblings who have chosen not to concern themselves with how much they make.

⌒ WHAT ABOUT YOUR KIDS? ⌒

Suppose you'd prefer that your children not end up with financial resources so unequal that they experience the jealousy, resentment, and worries described in this chapter. What should you do? According to sociologist Dalton Conley, the more children a family has, the more likely there are to be significant income disparities between the siblings as adults. His advice: If you don't want large gaps in income and achievement between your own children when they grow up—and if you want to maximize each child's odds of being successful—don't have more than two kids.

Chapter Seven

Rich Friend, Poor Friend

────────── ⟨⟩ ──────────

Nothing changes your opinion of a friend so surely
as success—yours or theirs.

—Franklin P. Jones

IN THE LATE 1990s, during the height of the dot-com boom,
we ran into an old friend, Jeff, who teaches at Stanford. We
asked how he was doing, and by way of answering, he
handed us the business section of *The New York Times* and
pointed to a story. The article was about an eighteen-month-
old company that had gone public the day before, and it
contained a picture of the company's three young founders—each now worth $150 million. Jeff pointed to one of
the founders and said "That's Alison Parker. Her husband
Dave and I are good friends. We teach together." And after
a pause Jeff added, "I'm spending the day fighting off
envy."

While few of us have friends with Dave and Alison's kind of money, it's still easy to identify with Jeff. We all have friends whose homes are nicer, whose kids have more of everything and who live more comfortably in every way, simply because they have greater financial resources.

Not that it's so hard to identify with Dave and Alison either. Even though most of us aren't gazillionaires, we all have friends whose resources fall short of our own and whose life styles are more modest—sometimes considerably so.

Just as Jeff and Dave want to continue to be friends, we'd like our friendships and family relationships to be unaffected by the wealth and income disparities that exist between us and the people we're close to. But ignoring the disparities isn't always easy, as the following letters reveal.

∼

*My rich friend keeps encouraging me to do things
I can't afford.*

When a friend is oblivious

Question: My old friend Pam is doing something that's really bugging me. She's always giving me suggestions like "Why doesn't Bob just take a cab?" when I gripe about how inconvenient it is for me to pick my husband up at the airport, or "Why don't you put a water feature in your yard? It would look lovely."

The answer to her questions is simple: because we don't have the money. Pam and her husband make much more than we do, and she just doesn't seem to get it that the reason Bob and I don't do these things is not because we lack the imagination, but because we can't afford to.

Am I overreacting here, or am I right that Pam is doing something really wrong? It's not as if she grew up with money, by the way—Pam and Dennis started making the big bucks only eight or ten years ago.

Answer: Mrs. Got Rocks, as they used to say, is being both foolish and unkind, and you'd be a candidate for sainthood if you weren't annoyed by her comments.

It sounds as if your old friend is too in love with her new lifestyle to pay any attention to yours. Shame on her. Maybe if you offered her a discount coupon for a dry cleaner or a car wash, it would remind her that what things cost was once an issue for her and remains one for you. But we doubt it. If you want Pam to stop, you're probably just going to have to tell her to cut it out.

I'd like my son's godparents to be wealthy.

Is it okay to choose a rich friend over a poor one?

Question: I plan to ask one of my two oldest friends to be the godmother of our first baby. Here's my problem: One friend's a successful lawyer married to a very successful businessman; the other's a divorced high school history teacher. I'm closer to my teacher friend, but I think in the long run having my rich friend as his godmother would be of greater benefit to my son. To be honest, she and her husband would be able to do more for Alexander. Am I horribly shallow to be thinking this way?

Answer: Well we wouldn't say "horribly."

Kidding aside, a godparent's principal responsibility traditionally has been to oversee the child's religious training, especially if the parents for some reason can't do it themselves. Of course, being a godparent is a social as well as a religious role, and you're by no means the first person to cast an appraising eye on the worldly advantages that having a particular person as his godparent might offer your offspring.

Unless you're misrepresenting to your lawyer friend your reasons for choosing her—say by encouraging her to believe it's her spirituality that matters—then what you're proposing is not unethical.

But let's talk for a moment about what you're not taking into account. What about Alexander's religious education? If that's of concern to you, then the relative ability of each of your two friends to provide it also needs to be considered. Also, is one of your friends more likely to develop a loving relationship with your son? Is one of them more likely to want to be involved in his life? And does one of them have more character—that is, when it comes to virtuous behavior, is one a better role model than the other?

Please understand, we don't assume and aren't suggesting that successful lawyers are morally flawed while high school history teachers are paragons of virtue. Indeed, it may be the lawyer is the better choice on every dimension. We simply want to caution you against becoming so distracted by the gifts and opportunities one prospective godmother can deliver that you fail to consider anything else.

⌒ **ALL GREAT FORTUNES BEGIN WITH A CRIME** ⌒

Do people in fact believe what this oft-quoted sentiment implies: that the rich are less ethical than the poor?

To find out, we asked the participants in our survey who they thought were more ethical: rich people or poor people. Here are their responses:

PERCENT WHO SAY

Rich people more ethical	3%
Poor people more ethical	27%
No difference between them	70%

Source: Fleming & Schwarz survey.

Individuals with the lowest incomes were most likely to assign virtue to the poor, while those with the highest incomes were most likely to say there is no difference between the two groups.

They pick the fancy restaurant, and we're stuck with half the tab for an overpriced meal.

When rich friends want to spend more than you do

Question: My wife and I are good friends with another couple. We go out to dinner with them every few weeks, and we always split the check fifty-fifty. Recently our friends inherited a lot of money, and now when we go out they only want to go to fancy restaurants. Thanks to their newfound appreciation for fine wine, the checks at these places routinely hit $350 to $400, or about double what the four of us used to spend. Every now and then, when the tab is really high, they make it a point to pick up the check. Even so, isn't it wrong for them to insist on going to such expensive places?

Answer: Absolutely. When friends go out together, they need to accommodate one another's budgets as well as their tastes. Your friends' occasional picking up a check doesn't get them off the hook for the lack of consideration they are showing you.

Given how distracted they seem to be by the excitement of spending their windfall, you are going to need to tell them directly that you'd like to go to restaurants where the tab is not likely to be more than $100 per couple (or whatever figure you feel comfortable with). These don't sound like folks who will take a hint.

We want to move, but our roommate can't afford to.

When you start to make a lot more money
than a close friend

Question: Three of us rented an apartment together in Manhattan after graduating from Harvard last year. Ross and I work in the securities industry, while Max takes odd jobs like bartending to supplement what he makes pursuing his career in digital music. Since our income is a lot higher than Max's, and since we're all good friends, Ross and I pick up most of the tabs when the three of us go out. But now Ross and I are thinking about moving to a nicer apartment, and we don't know what to do about Max. We know he can't afford a rent increase, and, as much as we like him, neither of us wants to pay his share. What should we do?

Answer: You and Ross have been very nice to subsidize Max's social life, and you shouldn't feel guilty about moving to nicer digs and not bringing Max along. Look at it this way: If Max cared as much about his home as his career, he would look for a job in a higher paying industry. What he can't do is have it both ways—the excitement of the music industry and the standard of living of the securities industry.

Not that anything you say suggests he expects to. Rather it's you and Ross who sound a bit uncomfortable with the fact that you two and Max are on divergent paths. But you shouldn't be. Differing paths don't mean you and Max can't be friends, only that you can't be the same kind of friends you were in college and that you're struggling to remain right now. The simple truth is that money is about to play an increasingly important role in your lives, and—while you can continue to treat Max to nights on the town and enjoy his company—there's not much you can do to eliminate the gap that's emerging between you.

Not that Max is doomed to the life of a pauper. On the contrary, if he succeeds in his field, he could one day be moving into a Malibu beach house while feeling equally saddened to be leaving you and Ross behind.

⌒ THE HAVES AND THE HAVE-NOTS ⌒

How prosperous do we consider ourselves to be? In a recent survey, the participants were asked: "Which of these groups are you in: the 'Haves' or the 'Have-nots'?"

Here are their responses:

	PERCENT WHO ANSWERED
Haves	47%
Have-nots	38%
Neither	11%
Unsure	4%

Source: Pew Research Center for the People & the Press.

(continued)

Make no mistake about it. Disparity-in-wealth problems exist *within* these groups at least as frequently as between them. Just ask a surgeon with a high six-figure income how rich he feels around an investment banker with an eight- or nine-figure net worth—or a barista at Starbucks about the luxuries a taxi driver can afford.

Our point: Each group has its "Have-mores."

Should we accept this very large gift?

When wealthy friends want to treat you to something extraordinarily expensive

Question: A few years ago one of my best friends, a software engineer, made a fortune when the company he was working for went public. For over twenty years, Graham and his wife and my wife and I have taken vacations together, first to inexpensive Mexican resorts, later to Europe and the Far East, and more recently to some of the nicer golf destinations. Now Graham and his wife want us to return to Europe for a month and, as he puts it, "stay at all the luxury hotels and dine at all the four-star restaurants we only dreamed of going to when we were young." I'm a successful attorney, so it is not as if my wife and I don't have the money to take a trip like this. But as I told Graham, we are not so rich that we want to spend our money on $500 dinners and $2,000 a night hotel suites—not night after night. After thinking it over, Graham called back to say that he and his wife would really like "to do Europe in style" and that they would really like for us to join them. So, he said, they were inviting us to travel with them at their expense.

I'm not sure how I feel about this. We never treated Graham and his wife to anything particularly grand when, in years past, my income was greater than his. And, as you can imagine, my wife and I are having trouble accepting generosity of this magnitude from anyone. Call it pride. Call it self-respect. Call it an old-fashioned, Calvinist sense of self-reliance, but this just doesn't feel right. Is it?

Answer: Hey, what are friends for? And, seriously, what's money for? In treating you to a luxury vacation, your friends would simply be treating themselves to a trip they want to take in the company of their dear old traveling companions. At least that's how it sounds to us. We assume that if you suspected Graham of having a hidden agenda—of wanting to show off, for example, or of wanting to prove he has won some lifelong competition with you—you'd have mentioned it. But let's assume his only agenda is enjoying the pleasure of your company. In that context, there is nothing wrong with the *haves* of the world accepting the generosity of the *have-mores*—unless, of course, doing so is going to make you feel like a poor relation.

⌐— **MY PAL, THE MILLIONAIRE** —⌐

We don't get to choose our family: They are who they are. But friends are a little different. Friends we get to choose, and the fact is that many of us prefer friends who are a lot like we are when it comes to how much money they have.

According to social scientist Susan Weinger, this is a pattern that starts early in life. Her research shows that poor children are most likely to want to befriend other poor children, while middle-class children are most likely to be drawn to other middle-class children.

And how do both groups feel about rich kids? According to Weinger, they'd like to play with their toys.

Children and Disparities in Wealth:
WHY CODY CAN'T HAVE THE NEW XBOX

Sooner or later every child figures out that there are other families who have more money than theirs does. For some, the light goes on when the kid down the block shows off his $5,000 bike or when a classmate is sporting her second pair of new sandals in a month. For others, there is no single clarifying moment, but a slowly emerging awareness propelled by the staples of popular culture—television, the movies, and Web sites like YouTube, Facebook, and Zebo.

All parents know they need to talk to their children about sex at some point. And most understand they need to teach their kids some fiscal responsibility ("If you spend it all now, you won't be able to buy anything later"). But what few parents explain to their children, except in the most cursory way, is why some of their kids' friends spend Christmas in Hawaii while others stay home and play video games on three-year-old consoles. That's too bad, because wealth gaps are an important fact of life.

So what should you say in a chalk talk on why Emma has a pony and Olivia has a poster of a pony?

Not that money doesn't matter, because it does. And not that people who care about money are shallow, because they're not. They're smart. Only when money is the *only* thing a person cares about is there a problem.

Look, children are going to need to think about money throughout their lives. If they're to do so wisely, it doesn't help to encourage them to believe that reflection and analysis about earning, saving, and spending the stuff are bad for the soul.

We can't prove this, but we'd bet that children who are taught that money doesn't or shouldn't matter often grow up to be the moochers, deadbeats, and freeloaders who cause so much trouble for their friends and relatives. To put it another way, children who haven't been taught respect for money are unlikely to show much respect for other people's money. Instead, they'll find it easy to feel superior to the people whose resources they expect to help themselves to.

All of which leads us to suggest that, rather than trying to ease the sting of wealth disparities by pretending that money isn't important, it makes better sense to explain to children why some of the people they know have so much money and others do not. Explain, for example, that Taylor's mother went to law school and is now a partner in a large law firm, where she works long hours, but earns hundreds of thousands of dollars a year. Or, that the Stewarts both work for the state, which means their salaries are relatively modest, but they have great benefits and considerable job security. Or that Timothy loves to ski, so he works as a waiter at a winter resort. It doesn't pay much, but he's happy—even though he knows he'll have to move on if he wants to live more comfortably and have some security.

Of course there are other possibilities: Cousin Bobby makes a lot of money selling drugs, but what he does is both illegal and immoral, and he's likely to end up in prison. Dad's friend Winthrop didn't earn his money; he inherited tens of millions from his father. And Rosa, who works for the cleaning service, is a recent immigrant whose lack of education and poor English make it difficult for her to earn more than the minimum wage.

Okay, we're oversimplifying. But our point remains: Wealth and income disparities aren't a mystery. They're something parents can and should explain to their children.

Specifically, by the time they enter high school, children should understand:

- That some jobs pay much more money than others;

- That the best-paying jobs generally require more education and training;

- That the best-paying jobs are almost always held by ambitious people who are willing to work hard; and

- That how much money people end up with as adults is directly linked to the choices they make—to savings and spending decisions as well as to career decisions.

Of course there are plenty of other factors that play a role in the income people earn and the wealth they achieve, not the least of which are good fortune and bad. But even so, children need to understand that many of the income and wealth disparities that they're going to experience as adults will be at least in part of their own making.

Don't get us wrong. We're not suggesting that kids be encouraged to think about everything solely in terms of money. Far from it. But what they need to learn is that, as our grandparents used to say, it doesn't grow on trees.

Was it wrong to lie to our friends about my husband's bonus?

When people exaggerate how much money they have

Question: My husband and I are close friends with another couple. These people are very successful—he's a bigshot investment fund manager, she's a much sought-after interior designer. We do pretty well ourselves, but we're not in their league. Recently my husband got a nice bonus at work, a bonus we encouraged our friends to believe was significantly larger than it really was. Now I feel very uncomfortable about this. Did we do anything seriously wrong?

Answer: Well if you were characters in an early-twentieth-century novel, you'd be in for a comeuppance.

As you know, the core ethical problem here is that you've lied. And it's not as if you lied to protect someone's feelings, say, or to give cover to a friend in a tight spot. You lied to impress people—people who, as close friends, have particular reason to believe they can trust what you say.

Is this seriously wrong? No. "Seriously wrong" would be if you lied about the size of that bonus in order to qualify for a loan.

Still, you're on a slippery slope. Once you begin to lie to your friends, what's to stop you from claiming to have eaten at expensive restaurants you've never been to or from referring to a high-status person you barely know as if he were a close friend—from, in short, taking advantage of your friend's trust to misrepresent who you are?

Certainly you wouldn't want them to do this to you. Which means that, instead of feeling "uncomfortable," you should be feeling remorseful—and determined not to let it happen again.

ᔥ "AS I WAS TELLING THE CEO ᔥ JUST THE OTHER DAY . . ."

One out of ten people say they've misled friends and family by making their job seem more impressive than it really is.

Source: *Money* survey.

We can't afford to return a favor.

When you need to reciprocate a rich friend's
generous hospitality

Question: A good friend of mine is in the process of taking over his father's real estate development business, which means he now has a great deal of money. Terry also has a fifty-foot sailboat on which my wife and I frequently are guests—not just for the day, but often for the weekend and occasionally for a week-long cruise. Here's the problem: We make a decent living, but there is no way we can reciprocate this kind of hospitality. What should we do?

Answer: Stop thinking you can't reciprocate, because you can. Your obligation is not to treat your friend to something of equal value, but to treat him to something thoughtful that he'll enjoy. Maybe that's a night at the opera, maybe it's a day at a ball game or maybe an afternoon at a spa. Whatever you know Terry would enjoy.

The point here is not that you need to match Terry's hospitality dollar for dollar. Rather it's that the disparity in your resources doesn't free you from your obligation to entertain Terry as thoughtfully as he's been entertaining you.

Wealth Gaps Between Friends
IT'S NOT JUST ABOUT THE MONEY

Wealth brings with it more than just the things that money can buy.

Here's what we mean (and please give us a moment to explain): Think of any small group whose members have never met before—the parents of kindergarteners joining forces for the first time to plan a bake sale, for example, or neighbors in a brand-new condo development coming to the first homeowners' meeting to elect a board, or perhaps a jury charged with reaching a verdict.

How hard is it to predict which parents, which neighbors, or which jurors will emerge as the leaders of these groups? Not as hard as you might think.

Research has shown, for example, that in a group of twelve people who've just met, three people are likely to do about half of the talking, six people are likely to do the rest, and the remaining three people are likely to say virtually nothing.

It's not difficult to predict who those three leaders will be—to identify in advance the individuals who will contribute the most to the discussion and who will have the greatest influence on the group's decisions. That's because, in situations like these, people almost always quickly cede the leadership of the group to the members with the highest status. Practically speaking, this means the individuals with two things: the most education and the most money.

Why care? Because this means that where a gap in wealth exists between friends, gaps in status and influence exist as well. And where gaps in wealth can occasionally become an issue in a friendship or a family, gaps in status are different. They get played out over and over in everyday situations.

Imagine, for example, you've made a bundle in real estate. A good friend owns a printing business and lives well, but not nearly as nicely as you. While he's made his peace with the gap in your resources, imagine how he must feel when the two of you are together and, simply because you have significantly higher status, others are much more interested in your thoughts than in his—even on topics about which your friend clearly knows more than you.

Or consider the opposite side of the coin: You've wanted nothing to do with the rat race and are happy running your boat and bait shop. An old friend, who happens to be a successful contractor, visits. It's always a pleasure to see him, but frankly you're not that interested in his many opinions on politics and the economy, so you tend to change the subject whenever he brings them up. In doing so, you are not showing him the deference he's become accustomed to receiving from people of your status. And trust us, at some level he is noticing this, the depth of your friendship notwithstanding.

Is anyone doing anything unethical in these situations? No. Is there an ethical justification for deferring to people whose status comes from their wealth? Of course not. But this is how the world works, and—if you want to have successful relationships with friends and relatives who have a lot more or a lot less money than you—it's worth keeping it in mind. Because being oblivious to who does and doesn't have the bucks and what status they're accorded as a result is a good way to wind up offending a friend.

Chapter Eight

When Gifts Come with Strings

————————— ⟳ —————————

There's no such thing as a free lunch.
—Economists' aphorism

Your grandfather lends you the money you need to start your business, but tells you that you have to give your cousin a job.

You give your son and daughter-in-law $300 and tell them to buy their son some nice clothes for the big family wedding, but instead they use the money to buy him the bike he wanted.

A friend asks to use your vacation home, and you say "fine." But she seems annoyed when you add that you'd like her to water the shrubs while she's there.

Sound familiar? Where there are gifts, loans, and favors, strings are often attached. Some of them are explicit ("I'll lend you the hundred bucks if you'll introduce me to Kirsten's sister"). And some of them are implicit ("What do you mean I can't borrow your car? I lent you the money to get it fixed").

More important, strings can be trouble—trouble because the gift- or loan-giver and the gift- or loan-recipient disagree over one of these four, sure-to-be-unsettling issues:

- Whether attaching a string at all is fair ("If it comes with a string, it's not a real gift" versus "Seven hundred and fifty bucks seems like a pretty real gift to me").

- Whether a particular string is unfair ("My mother shouldn't be insisting that if I want the loan I have to stop smoking—she knows how hard it would be for me to quit" versus "My daughter's never going to give up cigarettes without an incentive, and I'm worried about her health").

- Whether it's necessary to honor an arguably unreasonable string ("It wasn't fair of them to make me promise to save the money for school, so I didn't" versus "If he felt that way, he shouldn't have accepted our check").

- Whether it's necessary to honor a "hidden string"—a condition on a gift or loan you didn't know existed ("If I'd realized he was going to expect me to help him repaint his house, I'd never have asked for a loan" versus "If I'd realized he was unwilling to do a favor for *me*, I'd never have lent him the money").

The following pages look at these issues—and more.

∼

My parents want to stick me with my sister as a housemate.

When a loan you need comes with a string you hate

Question: My parents have offered to lend me the money for the down payment on a loft I love. But there's a catch. I'd have to let my younger sister live with me until she graduates from art school. Maggie's okay, but I don't want her for a roommate. She's a slob, her friends are obnoxious, and I hate the music she's always playing. I can't afford the loft without my parents' help, but I think it's unfair for them to stick me with Maggie. Do you agree?

Answer: Well, we certainly wouldn't want to be stuck with Maggie either. But that doesn't mean your parents are being unfair—or unreasonable.

Strings on loans have an undeservedly bad reputation. Far from being the antithesis of generosity, a string—or, more precisely, the opportunity to attach one—often makes the difference between someone's being willing or unwilling to make a loan or a gift. For your parents, the condition that your sister live with you may be a practical matter: Perhaps they can't afford to both lend you the money and pay

Maggie's rent someplace else. Or it may be philosophical: Perhaps they think you're too young to live on your own, or—alternatively—perhaps they're counting on you to have a civilizing influence on your sister. Whatever the reason, Maggie isn't a "catch" from your parents' perspective. She's an integral part of a generous offer they probably wouldn't otherwise be making.

More generally, there's nothing wrong with strings per se—not when they're announced up front and when they're clearly not cruel or capricious. After all, if you don't like the string, you can always say no to the loan.

For your sake, we hope you can persuade your parents to drop this particular string. But if they won't, then you simply have to decide whether getting something you'd really like to have is worth putting up with something you'd really like to avoid.

↷— ARE STRINGS FAIR? —↶

Eighty-five percent of the public agree:

"It's not fair to attach a 'string' to a gift of money—you should either give the money without any conditions or not give it at all."

Source: *Money* survey.

On this issue, 85 percent of the public happen to be wrong. There's absolutely nothing wrong, unfair, or unethical about

(continued)

making a gift or a loan conditional on the recipient's getting a job, for example, or coming home for the holidays. Only when strings are capricious, deviously manipulative, or exploitative of desperation are they unethical. As we pointed out to the prior letter writer, if someone objects to a string, that person can always say no to the money.

But be forewarned: If you give money to a friend or relative with the proviso that he or she, say, start looking for a job or stop gambling, the chances are very good that the beneficiary of your generosity will think you're being unfair.

Dad's trying to control the family from his grave.

When a will contains a string

Question: My father, who was a very successful writer, died recently. According to his will, $2,000,000 is to be placed in trust for his four grandchildren, two of whom are my sons (Mom died before Dad). According to the terms of the trust, each grandchild will receive their quarter of the trust when they turn twenty-five, provided that they've earned a college degree and that they've never attended a private school or college. Dad intended the first provision to give each of his grandchildren a big incentive to get an education, and I'm sure it will have that effect. The second provision, however, reflects his narrow-minded (in my opinion) prejudice that private schools do nothing but perpetuate an elite that has no place in a democratic society. To me, this restriction seems very unfair.

My oldest son, who's also the oldest grandchild, has a good chance of being admitted to an Ivy League college. As much as I loved my father, I don't see why Jonathan should pass up the opportunity to get that kind of an education just because Dad was an old-fashioned class-warrior. So here's my plan: My sister and I are the trustees of the trust my father established, and she has two kids who have the potential to be admitted to good colleges as well. I think that she and I should make a pact to give each child their quarter of my father's estate when they turn twenty-five, regardless of where they went to college. A lawyer's told me that when the court and the IRS review the distribution of assets in the trust, all they're going to look at are the numbers. So long as we give each grandchild one-quarter of Dad's estate and file the appropriate papers, no one will know or care where the kids went to college.

I know what I'm proposing is not completely above-board. But I think it's fairer than Dad's will, and my real concern here is to do right by my children. What do you think?

Answer: We think the $2,000,000 was your father's to do with as *he* wished, not as you wish. To subvert his will as you propose would be dishonorable—doubly so since, in appointing you and your sister trustees, he counted on you to carry out his wishes. If you're not prepared to do so, you should resign as trustee, not plot against the trust you have an ethical and legal obligation to uphold.

Not that we share your father's philosophy. We don't.

But he's entitled to his opinion and entitled to have it reflected in his will. To repeat, it's *his* money.

Besides, it's not as if a quality college education is available only at private institutions. If your son is forced to choose between, say, four years at Dartmouth with no inheritance and four years at Berkeley with half a million dollars waiting for him a few years later, we don't see how you can call that unfair.

On the chance we haven't persuaded you, consider this: Wills are public documents. Anyone in your family, any friend or neighbor, and any fan of your father's is free to review his. And rest assured, a few buttinskies have and will. If your son attends a private college, it won't go unnoticed. Award him an inheritance for which he's not qualified, and you run the risk of your action being brought to the attention of the court, the IRS, and possibly the district attorney.

Then there's the risk you run of your sister failing to honor the deal you've cooked up should your kids go to private schools and her children don't. After all, pacts—especially secret, illicit pacts—are easily broken. We know. Your sister would never go back on her word. But just remember: There's a reason *King Lear* has remained timely for four hundred years.

Still intent on carrying out your conspiracy and subverting the trust? Then think of the lesson you'll be teaching your children if you go forward with your plan, namely: If a disagreeable hurdle stands before you in life, see if you can't sneak around it.

Come on. You can do better than that.

Paying off my sister's credit card debt was not the good deed I had in mind when I gave her my car.

When a relative sells a gift from you

Question: My sister Carrie and her husband always seem to be struggling financially. Making matters worse, an uninsured motorist recently totaled Carrie's car, forcing her to take two buses to get to work. My wife and I had an old Honda in good condition that we were getting ready to trade in on a new one. But instead of trading it in, we gave the car to Carrie. Now I find out that she sold the Honda and used the money to pay off her credit cards, and I'm mad as hell.

It cost my wife and me an extra $3,500 to buy a car without the trade-in—a sacrifice we were willing to make in order to make it easier for my sister to get to work. But what we never intended to do was give Carrie and her husband $3,500 to pay off VISA, just so they can run up their balance again, as they're sure to do.

My wife says it's none of our business what Carrie did with the car after we gave it to her. But I think my sister was dead wrong. Was she?

Answer: When couples give their children cars, they often attach a string or two along the lines of "No racing," "You have to share it with your sister," or "You can keep it as long as your grades don't go down." While it's a lot less common to hand the keys and pink slip to an adult sibling and say "It's yours for this purpose only," there's absolutely nothing unethical about doing so. But generally speaking, the string has to be spelled out. So unless you told Carrie that the car was for her to use and not to be sold, she's done nothing unethical.

Still, Carrie was pretty insensitive. Out of courtesy, she should have spoken to you before selling the car. And once she heard your thoughts, she should have kept it—out of respect for your generosity and to stay on the good side of a big-hearted brother.

We hope Carrie's thoughtless behavior won't discourage you from similar acts of kindness in the future. But now you know: The next time you get the urge to help your sister, you'd better bulletproof your good deed to be sure it has the effect you have in mind.

↣ THE TIES THAT BIND ↢

One out of six people say they've had a lot of trouble with a friend or relative over a string attached to a gift or a loan. And four out of ten say they've run into some trouble.

Source: *Money* survey.

I made the down payment on my daughter's new house, but I'm not welcome to stay there.

When accepting a gift means incurring an unwanted obligation

Question: Last year, when my daughter and her husband asked me if I could help them buy their first home, I gave them the money they needed to make a down payment. Page and her family are now settled in it, and I've been planning a trip to see them. But now Page tells me I can't stay in their home. She says it would be "too stressful" for her, and I'm both angry and hurt. My daughter was happy to take my money, but apparently she can't take my company for a week. I think that, in accepting my gift of tens of thousands of dollars for that house, Page and her husband have an obligation to welcome me into it as a guest. What do you think?

Answer: We think your point is well-taken.

Your daughter and her husband can't have it both ways: If they're close enough to accept a five-figure cash gift from you, they're close enough to have you as their houseguest now and then.

The fact is, accepting a gift always places you in the debt of the gift-giver to some degree. Just because the gift-giver hasn't said "You owe me" doesn't mean you don't.

We can hear your daughter's protest: "But it's not a gift if it comes with an obligation." Nonsense. Not only do gifts always create an obligation on the part of the recipient, but the obligation is all the greater when the recipient solicits the gift, as Page did. If she didn't want to accommodate your easily anticipated desire to stay in their new house, she shouldn't have asked you to make the down payment on it.

Sometimes, of course, gift-givers expect too much in return. But unless there's something you've failed to mention—say, you never go anywhere without your 120-pound Bernese Mountain Dog—your expectations are not out of line.

*My aunt thinks I ran roughshod over her wishes,
and she's furious.*

When a gift of money is earmarked for a specific purpose

Question: My favorite aunt sent our twin boys $100 each for
their tenth birthdays, along with a note encouraging them
to buy themselves something they would really enjoy. Since
my husband and I are trying to teach our sons to save, we
told them to spend half the money and save the rest. When
my aunt heard what happened, she was really annoyed with
me. She said she'd made it clear that she wanted the boys
to spend the money on a treat, and we had no right to ignore her wishes. I think that parents have not only the
right, but the responsibility, to decide what gifts are appropriate for their kids, and that we did nothing wrong. Am I
right?

Answer: Of course parents must oversee the gifts their children receive. And had your aunt given each twin $1,000—
or a pit bull puppy—there would have been good reason for
you to become involved in the disposition of the gift. But a
present of $100, while certainly substantial, is not at a level
that requires parental intervention.

Had you encouraged your boys to spend more of their
birthday money on books and less on candy, your behavior
would have been in bounds. But unless your aunt has been
slipping them a Franklin every full moon, you were wrong
to insist that they save half.

Your aunt's gift to your children was *spending* money. If

she had wanted to be part of an object lesson on savings, she would have said so. And if you wanted her to be part of that object lesson, you should have spoken to her about it instead of unilaterally overriding her wishes.

The point here is that when a gift comes with strings attached—and especially when the gift is money—you can't simply keep the gift and disregard the strings, no matter how worthy your motive.

My Son Is Stealing My Grandchild's Money

Grandmom gives the new baby a Bratt Décor crib. Grandpa gives him a check for $500.

Mom's Aunt Debbie gives the baby a teddy bear. Dad's Uncle Barry gives him a check for $50.

Mom's friends Heather and Kimberly give the baby a Baby Gap gift card. Her friends at work give him an envelope containing two crisp hundred-dollar bills.

What's the difference between the crib, the teddy bear, and the gift certificate on the one hand and the three gifts of money on the other? The only items the baby's parents can easily appropriate for themselves are the checks and the cash.

Do parents really do that? You bet. Sometimes not only is it fine with the gift-givers, it's what they had in mind all along. Other times, though, they're shocked and angry. And with good reason.

Here's a typical scenario: Every year on his birthday and at Christmas, his grandparents give young Ethan $500 for his college education. But instead of putting the money into an account for him, Ethan's parents, who both have good jobs, have been using it for household expenses. They say that it's their responsibility to see that Ethan gets an education, that all of the family's money is in one "pot," and that it makes no difference whether these checks go for tuition or groceries.

Do they have a point? Sure, but not a very compelling one. For starters—and as we've already observed—when a gift of money comes with the stipulation that it be used for a specific purpose, it's not ethical to keep the gift and ignore the stipulation. So at the very least, Ethan's parents should check with the grandparents before diverting the cash to their own pockets.

And then there are Ethan's rights. Unless his grandparents agree to drop the string, the money isn't for the family pot; it belongs to Ethan. Just because he's not old enough to object when Mom and Dad use the money to pay household bills doesn't make it okay for them to appropriate what's rightfully his.

There's more than principle at stake here. As a practical matter, lots of things could prevent Ethan's parents from being able to pay for his education—a divorce, a layoff, or old-fashioned poor judgment, to name but a few. However honorable their intentions, his parents have compromised Ethan's prospects for a college education by, in effect, giving themselves an unsecured loan from his college fund.

If Ethan's family were desperately poor, that would change things. But in the situation we're describing, Ethan's parents aren't desperate, they're just unconcerned about the distinction between their son's money and their own, as well as indifferent to the feelings and intentions of generous relatives.

So what can you do if you find yourself in Ethan's grandparents' shoes? Open a 529 Plan for the child with a bank, stock brokerage firm, or mutual fund company—an account that only you will have control of until he needs the money for his education. Then, in the future, tell him each time you stow away some money in it.

⌒— PULLING THE STRINGS —⌒

Imagine that your parents offer to lend you the money you need to buy a car, but only on the condition that you stop trying to be a writer and return to law school. Do you think it's fair for them to attach this string to the loan? And if you accept the loan, are you obligated to return to law school?

If you're like most people, your answer to the first question is no. Sixty-three percent of the respondents to our survey said they didn't think it was fair for the parents to attach a return-to-school condition to the loan.

But if they accepted the money, what then? While the vast majority of the participants—almost three out of four—felt they'd be "absolutely" obligated to return to school if they accepted their parents' money, 19 percent said that only "maybe" would accepting their parents' money obligate them, and 9 percent said they'd feel no obligation to return to school.

(continued)

So lenders take note: If the deciding factor leading you to lend someone money is the opportunity to attach a condition to the loan—a condition you believe to be in the best interests of the borrower—remember this: There's about one chance in ten that the person to whom you lend the money will feel absolutely no obligation to abide by the condition you impose. And there's better than one chance in four that the borrower will feel it's up to them whether they must honor that condition.

Source: Fleming & Schwarz survey.

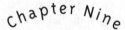

Chapter Nine

Promises, Promises

⸻ ⌘ ⸻

Magic trick: To make people disappear, ask them to fulfill their promises.

—Mason Cooley

A friend with whom you go antiquing promises you that if she ever decides to sell the wonderful lamp you helped her find, you can have it for the price she paid. Then, a year later, she sells it for a bundle on eBay without saying a word to you.

Your husband left you all his money in return for your promise that, in turn, you would leave the money to his alma mater. But you're disappointed by changes at the school, and you realize there are other institutions you'd prefer to support.

An old friend promises that if you let him stay in your mountain cabin for the summer, he'll replace the rotting boards on the back deck. But midway through the project—the point at which the deck is torn apart and can't be used until the new boards go in—your friend meets the woman of his dreams and follows her to Maui.

In a perfect world, no one would make—or ask for—a promise that could prove difficult to keep. But in the real world, promises can be extremely difficult to keep and awfully tempting to break—so tempting, in fact, that most of us employ a psychological trick to let ourselves off the hook. Here's how it works: When someone else breaks a promise, we typically assign their bad behavior to their character. But when we break a promise, we tend to say it was only fair given the circumstances that emerged since the promise was made.

In other words, when others break promises to us, we think they're not being very nice ("If Susan weren't so greedy, she'd have sold me the lamp like she promised"). But when we break a promise, we tell ourselves it's due to circumstances beyond our control ("I wanted to let Karen have the lamp, but I knew I'd get much more for it on eBay, and I really need the money").

Then there's the unfortunate ease with which unrealistic promises can be made when there's an incentive to do so. As François, duc de La Rochefoucauld, a seventeenth-century writer known for his witty observations on human foibles, noted, "We promise in proportion to our hopes."

That's why your brother-in-law, who wants to open a restaurant, believes he'll have no difficulty repaying the loan he is asking you for. Or why your son says if you buy him an iPod, he'll walk the neighbors' dogs and shovel the snow off their sidewalks until he's made enough to pay you back. They promise in proportion to their hopes.

And what are the odds of these promises being kept? To again quote La Rochefoucauld, "We deliver in proportion to our fears."

~

I promised Mom she could always stay in her home.

When a promise is difficult to keep

Question: Ten years ago, my elderly mother gave my husband and me the money we needed to buy a beautiful home in a place we'd always wanted to live. In return, we promised her we'd do whatever it took to see that she was able to spend the rest of her life in her own home. Now, however, Mom's health is failing, reliable live-in attendants are difficult to find—not to mention very costly for Mom— and we're spending all of our free time doing chores for her. Must we continue to honor our promise? I really think Mom would be happier—and safer—in an assisted-living facility.

Answer: Just what were you thinking when you made that promise?

We hope it wasn't that you'd do your best to keep your mother at home, but pack her off to an institution if it didn't work out. Because that wasn't the deal. Moreover, your mother didn't merely *try* to honor her end of the bargain you struck, she did honor it. She gave you the money.

So it's time for you to face the facts: Reneging on a promise because it has become difficult to keep is dishonorable. You may be telling yourself that when you made the promise you had no idea how tough keeping it would be. But any mature couple, as you and your husband must have been when you accepted your mother's check, should have been able to figure out that keeping an elderly widow in her own home could easily become as difficult and burdensome as it in fact has proven to be.

Of course we can imagine how tempting the dream home was. We can even imagine how your desire to live there could lead you to discount the myriad difficulties that keeping your word might very well lead to.

But none of this gets you off the hook. Even if it means spending some of the money you're hoping to inherit from your mother—or some of your own money, for that matter—even if it means moving out of your dream home and into her house so you can take care of her, the bottom line is this: If you want to have a clear conscience about the money you took from your mother, you're going to have to keep her in her own home until either she tells you that she wants to move or her doctor insists that she does.

⌒— KEEPING YOUR WORD—FOREVER —⌒

What would you do if you found yourself in the shoes of the woman who wrote the last letter? We asked the participants in the *Money* survey just that. Specifically, we told them to imagine themselves in a situation very much like hers and asked whether, in those circumstances, it would be wrong for them to insist that their mother move to an assisted-living facility.

Here are their responses:

PERCENT WHO SAY

Definitely wrong	34%
Probably wrong	39%
Probably not wrong	22%
Definitely not wrong	5%

Source: *Money* survey.

What these results say, loud and clear, is this: If you're a parent contemplating making this sort of a deal with one of your children, think long and hard before going forward. Yes, most people thought breaking the promise to Mom was at least probably wrong. But only one in three—one in three!—thought it was *definitely* wrong.

So unless you are completely confident that, when the chips are down, your child is certain to be one of the one in three, hang on to your money. You may need it to pay for full-time, in-home care.

Twenty years ago I swore to always look after my brother.

Is there ever a good reason to break your word?

Question: My parents died when I was in my early twenties. In their will, they left their entire estate to me and nothing to my older brother. However, they'd always made it clear that their money was for both of us and that they were counting on me to look after Adam, who has a learning disability as well as an anger management problem. I'd always promised my parents I'd do so, and that's what I've done. I'm in touch with my brother every week, and, when he's not working, I give him a check for what he needs. Meanwhile, I've never taken any of my parents' money for myself or my family.

Adam and I are both in our thirties now, and lately I've begun to feel that continually doling out our parents' money to him is doing more harm than good. He never lasts at a job because he says his employers are always "unfair" to him. He has a girlfriend who's obviously just sponging off him. And he's drinking too much, at least that's how it seems to me. I care about my brother, and I want to do what my parents expected of me. But I think Adam would be better off if he had to get up every day and earn a living like the rest of us. Plus at the rate I'm writing checks, there's not going to be any of my parents' money left for my family and me. What should I do?

Answer: People are responsible for keeping the promises they make—unless, that is, the promise was unfairly extracted. And that's what we'd say your parents did in making you agree when you were so young that you'd accept responsibility for your difficult brother.

Were you the age you are now when you were having those conversations with your folks, you might have known to ask them to divide their money between you and Adam and to leave his share in the care of a trustee—perhaps even someone other than you. Indeed, had your parents lived to see your brother's behavior as an adult, they might have chosen to provide for him through the vehicle of an annuity or have asked you to help him with money only in a true crisis. Instead, however, they effectively left everything to Adam, with you as an unpaid and, we'd bet, unappreciated trustee.

We can't believe your parents intended to put you in the position of subsidizing Adam's irresponsible behavior. And we doubt they intended you to spend your entire inheritance on his care.

Hence you can in good conscience tell your brother that he needs to take real responsibility for his own support. This doesn't mean abandoning Adam, of course. It just means no longer using all the money that belongs to both of you to bankroll his dysfunctional and self-destructive way of life.

We're expecting a baby, but our housemate won't move out because of a promise my fiancé once made.

When circumstances change

Question: Two years ago, when his employer was sending him to Ireland for a year, my fiancé Derek asked his best friend Jason if he'd like to live in Derek's home, so the house wouldn't be empty. Derek said Jason could stay there for $600 a month, which is about a third of what the rent should be. At first, Jason said no, because he really liked his apartment and he thought he'd be unlikely to get one as good when Derek returned. So to get Jason to stay, Derek gave him an even better deal. He told Jason he could stay in the house for as long as he wanted and pay only $500 per month in rent, and that's when Jason moved in.

I met Derek right after he returned from Ireland, and now we're expecting a baby. Since we're starting a family, we really need the whole house, but Jason refuses to move. He says he gave up his good apartment only because Derek promised him he could stay as long as he wanted.

I'm furious. I think our baby should take precedence over Derek's promise to Jason, which was made two years ago when circumstances were completely different. And I think Jason is being completely unfair in insisting on staying. What do you think?

Answer: We think you should take a few deep breaths and calm down.

Being pregnant gives you a claim to a seat on a crowded

bus, but not the moral authority to evict Jason. He is living in Derek's house for one reason only, and it's that Derek persuaded him to move in by promising him he would never have to leave.

While we agree that Jason should move, there is no getting around the fact that Derek is reneging on his half of the deal. This puts Derek—not Jason—a long way from the moral high ground.

The only thing that gets Derek off the hook here is that the promise per se was absurd. In fact, Jason, as well as Derek, was foolish to imagine that Derek could hold up his end of the bargain indefinitely. After all, most men marry. Most couples have children. And, whether or not they have children, most couples ultimately don't want roommates.

In other words, the deal was doomed from the start.

We don't know Derek's age, but we're assuming he was too young to know better when he made this naive agreement. That doesn't mean, though, that he can simply walk away from it. Since he's bailing out on his promise to provide Jason with a cheap home, Derek should offer to pay a substantial portion of Jason's rent for the next couple of years. Sure, that's a lot of money. But Jason *earned* his low-rent deal—he held up his end of the bargain. And don't forget, his moving out is entirely to your and Derek's benefit and his detriment. That's why you need to compensate him—for sacrificing his best interests (a great deal on rent) for yours (room for the baby).

False Promises, Wishful Thinking, White Lies, and More

When people make promises they know they're not going to keep, of course that's unethical. They're simply lying. But suppose they make a promise they're not sure they'll be able to keep. Is that unethical as well? The answer to that question and four like it—questions about everyday promises and everyday reasons to want to set them aside—follow.

Making a promise you know you might not be able to keep

Say you live in Boston, you're a big Red Sox fan, and your brother-in-law calls with a deal: Someone has given him a pair of great seats to tomorrow night's game, and he says he'll take you if you agree to come over on Saturday and help him paint his kitchen. You're supposed to work on Saturday, but you're confident you can find someone to cover for you, so you say sure. After all, your heart's in the right place, right?

Wrong. No matter how right the place your heart is in, it doesn't justify making a promise you're not certain you can deliver on. Explain to your brother-in-law the odds of your being available on Saturday, and you're in the clear. But accept his offer with only the hope—no matter how reasonable—that you can keep your promise, and you've put self-interest ahead of integrity.

Are promises to some folks more binding than promises to others? For example, is a promise to a close friend more

binding than a promise to a casual acquaintance? Or a
promise to a straight arrow versus a corner cutter? In other
words, does it matter to whom you've made the promise when
it comes to your obligation to keep it?

No, absolutely not. There is no meaning to giving your
word if the seriousness with which you do so depends on
your assessment of the worthiness of the recipient of your
promise. Breaking a promise to anyone compromises your
character. The character of the person to whom you've
made the promise is irrelevant. If you find yourself saying,
"I know I promised my cousin's kid a summer job, but why
should I hire her? What's her father ever done for me?"
you've gone over to the dark side.

When is a promise not a promise?

When it's a social convention. But promises involving
money almost never fall into that category. For example,
telling people you'll call them for lunch is, in most in-
stances, not a real promise. But telling them that you'll buy
them lunch is.

Are there circumstances related to when or how a promise was
made that make it okay to break your word?

Yes, but they are few and far between. Suppose an eigh-
teen-year-old extracts from his eighty-year-old grandmother
a promise that—in exchange for helping clear out her ga-
rage and basement—she'll give him her late husband's

baseball card collection, a collection that he knows is very valuable but she does not. That's a promise that needn't be kept. Individuals can't be held to their word when they didn't understand the implication of their promise and couldn't be expected to. In this case, Grandma thought she was promising her grandson a charming memento of his grandfather's life, not a collection worth hundreds if not thousands of dollars.

Can a change in circumstances make it okay to break a promise?

Sometimes yes, but mostly no.

When you make a promise as part of a bargain and the other person lives up to his or her side of the deal, only two types of changes in circumstance provide ethical grounds for reneging. One is when keeping the promise would un-equivocally mean doing more harm than good. Consider, for example, the woman a few pages back who promised her mother she could remain in her home for the rest of her life. If the mother's health fails to the point that her doctor says she must move to a facility providing medical care, the daughter is relieved of her obligation to keep her mother at home. On the other hand, if a financial adviser tells the daughter she'd be better off moving her mother to the same facility, the promise remains in effect. Doing no harm means doing no harm to the promise-receiver, not doing no harm to the promise-maker's bank account.

The only other change in circumstances that excuses breaking a promise is when a highly unlikely event occurs that leads to changes in your life you could not be expected to anticipate. For example, suppose you get a job by promising your boss, who's going to spend six months training you, that you'll stay at the job for at least two years. You're off the hook on that promise if your father dies unexpectedly and you need to move back home to help your family. But if you leave the job after only a year in order to follow your boyfriend to another city, you'll be leaving town without your honor.

Chapter Ten

What Are We Going to Do about Our Wills?

Money isn't everything. But it sure keeps you in touch with your children.

—J. Paul Getty

EIGHTY PERCENT OF the wealth held by American households comes from the money that flows within families from older generations to younger generations, according to economists Lawrence Kotlikoff and Lawrence Summers. While the media may focus on the outsize estates of people like Anna Nicole Smith, the fact is, inheritances play an important role in the economic well-being of most American families.

That's just one reason why individuals find it difficult to decide who gets what when they die: For most of their heirs, the money is really going to matter.

Then there's the symbolic meaning of the bequest: Many people believe the more you leave someone, the more you love them, and the less you leave someone, the less you care.

And finally, there are all the classic, family-specific dilemmas people face when they go to draw up their wills, among them:

- I have two children. One really deserves my money, and the other really needs it.

- I love my children equally, but one is married to a woman who loathes me, and I don't want her to get a dime.

- My daughter hasn't spoken to me in twelve years. I want to disinherit her, but I fear it would create a rift between her and my two sons, and I don't want that to happen.

It can be tough to prepare a will that satisfies the conflicting needs we feel as we line up the most important people in our lives and decide how to share our life's savings with them. Not that the folks on our short list wouldn't be happy to help us sort through our priorities.

$\sim$

Is it okay to leave more money to my son's kids than my daughter's?

When some grandchildren have less than others

Question: I'm a widower, and I need help deciding how to divide up my estate. Here's the situation: I have two children, a son and a daughter. My son has four children and my daughter has two. For a variety of reasons, I've decided to leave my money to my grandchildren. But there's a complication. Several years ago, my daughter's father-in-law died and left each of her children enough money to provide for their college educations. This leads me to wonder: Should I be leaving equal amounts to each of my six grandchildren, or should I leave less to the two who inherited from their other grandfather and more to the other four? I love all of my grandchildren equally, and I wouldn't want to do anything that suggested I didn't.

Answer: There's nothing wrong with weighing your grandchildren's other financial resources as you decide how to allocate your estate among them. But why is their wealth the only thing you're taking into account?

What about the devotion and service of each set's parents to you? Doesn't that matter?

And how about the love and attention you receive from each of your grandchildren? Doesn't it count?

Here's our point: Once you begin differentiating among people you love equally, you should be considering *all* the ways in which they are more or less deserving of your generosity, not measuring them on a single dimension.

And here's our advice: Before you prepare a will that leaves the bulk of your estate to your son's children, sit down with your daughter and explain your decision. She deserves to hear from you directly that the only reason her brother's family is being favored in your will is that you believe his children can use your money more than hers can. And she deserves the opportunity to tell you whether she thinks her father is being fair.

What's in Other People's Wills

When it comes to leaving money to their children, what do most people do? According to numerous studies, they split what they have equally among their children. About four-fifths of all estates are divided this way: Two children and the split is fifty/fifty; three and it's one-third/one-third/one-third; and so on.

But what about the one out of five parents whose bequests favor one child over another? Research by economists Audrey Light and Kathleen McGarry suggests that these folks are likely to have one of three things on their minds.

The first is a desire to reward the children who are most attentive to them or to whom they feel closest. For example, one daughter may do all the heavy lifting when it comes to caring for the parent, while her brothers show up only on Mom's birthday and Christmas. Given that caregiving is sometimes unevenly divided, it's no surprise that many parents decide to reward those children whose kindness and attention they rely on—their unconditional love for their other children notwithstanding.

The second reason parents make unequal bequests is to help a child who they believe needs money more than their other children do. Maybe the child has a disability that prevents him or her from working, or maybe the child simply isn't as prosperous as his or her brothers and sisters. Whatever the situation, some parents want to use their own wealth to equalize their children's financial fortunes.

The third reason some parents choose to leave unequal bequests has to do with the parents' biological relationship with their children—what Light and McGarry call the "evolutionary motive." Specifically, there are parents who leave less money to stepchildren and adopted children than to their biological children. And there are parents who leave more money to those of their children who have more biological children themselves. In other words, they reward the children who have given them the most biological grandchildren.

Our own research, conducted for *Money Magazine,* uncovered a fourth motive for leaving some children less, namely: parsimony. It appears people hate to think that the money that remains in their estate will be squandered by an improvident child, perhaps not only because their sensibilities are offended, but also because they worry that future generations will be deprived of any benefit from their hard-earned cash. So, aside from the belief that their estate should be evenly divided, the factor survey respondents were most likely to say mattered greatly to them was how responsible each child in the family was about money.

And how common is it for people to take their prospective heirs' fiscal responsibility into account when preparing a will? The table which follows shows the percent of respondents who rated each consideration listed as very important in deciding how much money to leave to each of their children (participants were free to rate as very important as many factors as they wished).

PERCENT WHO RATE EACH CONSIDERATION AS VERY IMPORTANT	
Treating each child exactly the same and dividing the money equally.	69%
How responsible each child is about money.	37%
How much each child has helped you.	29%
How close you are to each child.	22%
How much money each child has.	22%
How many children of his or her own each child has.	19%
Whether a child is biological or not.	14%
How you feel toward each child's spouse.	10%

Source: *Money* survey.

The only time we hear from our son is when he wants money.

Should you disinherit a child?

Question: My husband and I are having a disagreement over our wills. We have four children, and we'd always planned to divide our estate equally among them. But our son Kenneth has paid no attention to us for years. We get a card from him at Christmas and a phone call when he needs money. That's it. Our other three kids are a big part of our lives and help us out all the time.

My husband wants to leave Kenneth out of our wills. I'm not so sure. While I feel terribly wounded by his behavior, he is our flesh and blood. What should we do?

Answer: Our vote is to drop Kenneth.

As you decide how much money to leave each of your children, there's nothing wrong with taking into account how each of them has treated you. In fact, fairness to your three loving children requires that you not be blind to the love and loyalty they've shown you, as opposed to the contempt their brother has.

Do see a lawyer, though, and make sure the language of your wills protects your estate from any claim Kenneth might try to make. From what you've said, he sounds like the kind of guy who'd be only too happy to take a final shot at squeezing a few bucks out of his mom and dad.

∽— THAT'LL TEACH 'EM! —∾

One in ten parents do not name all of their children as beneficiaries of their will. In other words, 10 percent of parents disinherit at least one child.

Source: Thomas Dunn and John Phillips, *Economics Letters*.

Who should get my house?

When two relatives have equal claims on your generosity

Question: I'm a childless widow with two nephews whom I've been close to all their lives. They will be my sole heirs, but I'm not sure how to divide things between them. While I have some CDs, my principal asset is my home, which is worth close to $300,000. My inclination is to leave it to my nephew Tom—because he lives nearby, and he and his wife do a great deal for me. Also there are months when Tom and his wife struggle to make ends meet, and I know the house would put them on their feet.

However, I also want to be fair to my other nephew, Scott, who is Tom's cousin. Scott now lives out-of-state, so I don't see him very often. But he frequently calls, never forgets my birthday, and, in general, is very attentive. Scott's not wealthy, but he makes a good living as a salesman for a paper company, and he and his family live comfortably. While the money they'd get from the house if they inherited it would mean a great deal to them, it wouldn't help them out the way it would Tom.

Further complicating things, it was Scott's father—my brother, Bill—who gave my husband and me the money we needed to make the down payment when we bought the house forty years ago. Bill also helped us with the mortgage payments for a couple of months when my husband was out of work, and he replaced the hot water heater for us when our old one broke. I wouldn't be living in this house today if it weren't for my brother's generosity. I was never able to repay Bill when he was alive for all he did, which is why a big part of me wants to leave the house to Scott, his only child.

What should I do?

Answer: From what you've said, we see no reason why you should favor one nephew over the other. Tom's financial needs and kindness to you don't trump your debt of gratitude to Scott's father, or vice versa. You have very good reasons for leaving your home to both of your nephews, and that is what you should do.

There's something else you should do as well: Write a letter to your nephews, to be opened after your death, expressing your love for them and explaining why you've done what you've done. Joint ownership inevitably leads to a squabble or two, and one way to minimize their intensity is to be certain that Tom and Scott both understand that their loving aunt did her best to do right by them.

ᐁ TO HECK WITH THEM? ᐁ

How much do people worry about hurting the feelings of others when drawing up their wills? To find out, we asked the participants in our survey which of the following two statements they agreed with more:

- In drawing up their wills, people should leave their money to whomever they please and not worry about whose feelings may be hurt.

or

- In drawing up their wills, people should be careful not to hurt the feelings of their family and loved ones.

Here are their responses:

PERCENT WHO SAY

Leave money as you please.	78%
Don't hurt loved ones' feelings.	22%

(continued)

But those results tell only half the story. Look at the responses of the participants age seventy-five and older:

PERCENT WHO SAY

Leave money as you please.   54%

Don't hurt loved ones' feelings.   46%

Source: Fleming & Schwarz survey.

What's going on here? It appears that as people get older—and as preparing a will becomes less a just-in-case exercise and more a central part of their financial planning—what they think of others becomes relatively less important and what others will ultimately think of them becomes relatively more important. In short, seniors appear concerned that their legacy not be resentment.

Must I leave my money to the stepchildren I never see?

What do you owe someone from whom you inherit money?

Question: I was a widow with very little money when I met Sam, a widower. We fell in love, got married, and then lived in his home for twelve years before he died. The home was Sam's one real asset, and he left it to me. That was six years ago. About two years ago I sold the house for $400,000. I'm now in the process of updating my will, and here's the problem: I have three children from my first marriage, and so did Sam. My children and grandchildren are very much a part of my life, but Sam's children and grandchildren are not. They were attentive for the first year or two after Sam died, but we haven't remained close. I would like to leave all of my money to my own family. But the fact is, everything I have came from Sam. What's more, his children were raised in the house I inherited from him. What are my obligations to Sam and his family under these circumstances?

Answer: Nothing you've said suggests that Sam wished to disinherit his children and grandchildren, yet that's, in effect, what he did. Unless he was alienated from his family—and we assume you'd have told us if that were the case—our bet is that his love for you blinded Sam to the fact that leaving you everything could have the effect of transferring his family's resources to yours for the generations that follow. To put it another way, it sounds to us as if Sam's estate planning consisted solely of planning for you and that he either forgot about his children or counted on you not to.

Whatever the case, if Sam loved his family and they loved him, you should, in your will, share with them some of the wealth you inherited from him. Right now, they have nothing, and you have everything. While that's what Sam must have wanted, it doesn't mean that his family should never get any of his estate—that all that was his should go only to your children and grandchildren. Unless there are important details you've left out of your story—say, your stepchildren disapproved of their father's marriage to you and treated you badly—you should leave Sam's family at least half the money you inherited from him.

The Samaritan's Dilemma and the Equalizer's Dilemma

Having trouble—real trouble—trying to decide how much money to leave to each of your children? Perhaps you're facing either the Samaritan's Dilemma or the Equalizer's Dilemma.

What economists refer to as the Samaritan's Dilemma occurs when one or more of your children spends foolishly and fails to save in the belief that the less money they have, the more you'll feel compelled to leave to them. You hate the idea of endorsing this behavior, but what are you going to do, leave them penniless?

What we call the Equalizer's Dilemma takes the following form: You want to leave your money to your two sons, but—because one of them has more money than the other—you are uncertain what proportion to leave to each. On the one hand, you're considering leaving more to the son who has less, in order to even out your children's fortunes. On the other hand, one reason he has less is that he's lazy and irresponsible. So, if you leave more money to the child who has less, you'll be rewarding him for his indolent ways while in effect punishing his brother for his industry and prudence.

As with all dilemmas, the Samaritan's and the Equalizer's dilemmas come with no easy solutions, only a set of unappealing options. That said, these particular quandaries suggest a strategy—not for the individuals facing them, but for people who wish to avoid them—to wit: No matter how wealthy you are, teach your children to save!

∾— **IS ANYBODY HAPPY?** —∾

One out of three people have run into trouble with friends or family over the terms of their own will.

and

One out of twenty have had a lot of trouble on this score.

Source: *Money* survey.

Will-lessness

Only about one-third of adults have drawn up a will, according to a *Wall Street Journal* Online/Harris Interactive Personal Finance Poll.

What happens if you die without one? Your state legislature decides who gets your money. Or, to be more precise, your estate will be distributed in accordance with the laws of the state in which you reside. These laws favor the closest relatives of the deceased, generally placing spouses first, followed by children. (If you are single and childless, typically your parents come first, followed by your siblings.)

So if you don't have a will and you are separated but not divorced, it's quite possible that the rules of your state require all of your money go to the last person on earth you want to leave it to. Or, say, you have a niece with whom you're especially close or a beloved aunt who's lost all her money. Chances are these worthy beneficiaries are so far behind the relatives whom the state places at the head of the line that they will inherit nothing if you die without a will.

Our point: To be sure that your true wishes are carried out and that you're fair to the people whom you'd like to inherit your money, get a will.

Giving It Away Before You Go

The vast majority of parents, in leaving money to their children, leave an equal amount to each child. But how about the gifts of money that parents bestow on their children before they die? There the story is quite different. While only 20 percent of parents make unequal bequests to their children in their wills, economists have found that three-quarters of parents—75 percent—give unequal amounts of money to their children while they're still alive.

The question is, why? Why do most folks make equal bequests in their wills, yet give unequal amounts to their children while they're alive? Economists speculate that it's because bequests are public, while gifts need not be. In other words, fearing that unequal bequests could be interpreted as meaning, say, "I love Melinda more than the others," or "I'm leaving less to Oliver because he's no good," most parents opt for equality *über alles*.

Chapter Eleven

Beneficiaries and Their Great Expectations

Men sooner forget the death of their father than the loss of their patrimony.

—Niccolò Machiavelli

LOTS OF PEOPLE would like to know what their parents' or other relatives' passing might represent for them financially, and there's nothing necessarily unethical or unseemly about their curiosity. After all, if you're hoping to retire early but aren't sure if you can afford to, wouldn't you appreciate knowing what to expect from your parents' estate? Or if you had an elderly great-aunt with money, wouldn't you like to know if you might someday be seeing some cash from her that could help with your children's education?

Of course there's also nothing unethical about keeping your estate plans to yourself. In fact, there can be many good reasons not to reveal the details of your will to the people in it, not the least of which is the danger of setting off lobbying efforts, at best, and conflicts between your heirs, at worst.

Whatever their reasons, most parents, at least, choose not to lay their cards on the table. The survey we conducted for *Money* shows that only four out of ten adult children say they know what's in their parents' wills—that's four out of ten among children whose parents in fact have a will. And only one out of six children has actually read the document. But that doesn't keep most of the others from wondering, hoping, and occasionally scheming.

~

My sister thinks she'll be on Easy Street when Dad dies.

When your sibling is counting on an inheritance you know is unlikely

Question: My sister, who's always been kind of extravagant, is convinced our father has lots of money, and that when he dies, she'll be rolling in dough. I'm close to Dad, and I know that his assets are much more modest than Sandra imagines. Also, he's quite old now, and his living expenses are increasing (for example, someone comes in every day to help with chores and meals). The problem is that Sandra, counting on a big inheritance, spends the money she earns very foolishly. My father hasn't chosen to reveal his finances to her, but I'm wondering: Does that mean that I'm prohibited from giving my sister a heads-up, so that she'll slow down her spending?

Answer: Well, there's a twist. Sometimes parents lead their adult children to believe they have less money than they actually do in order to get the kids to start saving. But in the situation you describe, either your father has sent the opposite message to your sister, or your sister doesn't understand the information she's getting.

You are, of course, obligated to keep private the specific information your father has shared with you about his finances. But unless you suspect that your father has intentionally chosen to create a false impression with your sister (in which case you should be having a talk with him about what's happened as a result), there's nothing wrong with your explaining to your sister in general terms that your dad is not a wealthy man and that he's drawing down his savings to pay for his in-home care.

We're not convinced that this information will lead your sister to change her behavior. But at least you'll know that, however Sandra chooses to spend her money, she's not acting under the mistaken belief that she's going to be coming into a fortune.

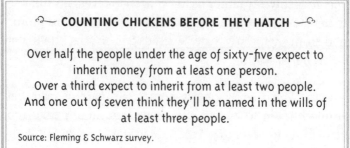

∽— **COUNTING CHICKENS BEFORE THEY HATCH** —∾

Over half the people under the age of sixty-five expect to
inherit money from at least one person.
Over a third expect to inherit from at least two people.
And one out of seven think they'll be named in the wills of
at least three people.

Source: Fleming & Schwarz survey.

I told Dad not to leave money to my daughter.

When your child discovers you persuaded your father to
change his will

Question: When my father was revising his will a couple of
years ago, he told me that he was going to leave $150,000
to each of my two children. I told him I thought that was
wonderful, but I urged him to stipulate that my daughter
Stephanie wasn't to receive the money until her thirtieth
birthday. Although she was twenty-one years old at the
time, Stephanie—unlike her sister Amanda—was still very
foolish about money, and I was worried she would just blow
this very large gift.

Dad did as I requested, and when he died this year,
Amanda got her $150,000 outright, and Stephanie got her
$150,000 in trust. Stephanie realizes that I had a hand in
this, and she's furious at me for meddling. She claims that
it was wrong for me to persuade my father to treat her dif-

Our brother is stealing our inheritance.

When your mother is letting one child borrow against future bequests

Question: My mother has divided her estate equally among her three children. The problem is my brother has "borrowed" several times against his future share, but nobody's written anything down, which seems to be okay with Mom. I know it's her money, but don't my sister and I have any rights here? We feel like we're going to be cheated when she dies and there's no record of the money our brother owes her.

Answer: To cut to the chase: Is it your mother's intention that the money she's been giving your brother counts against his share of her estate, or has it been a de facto gift?

If she believes the money is to be repaid—and there's no way of knowing unless you ask her directly—then what's going on is terribly unfair to you and your sister. You should immediately start working with your mother and, if he's willing, your brother to prepare a list of the loans she's made to him (checkbooks and bank statements will help). Your mom also needs to make certain her will includes language that lays out how the outstanding loans are to be treated.

If your mom views the money as a gift, though, that's a different story. As you say, it's your mother's money, which means it's hers to do with as she likes for the most part. While there's nothing wrong with telling your mother

ferently than he treated her sister, and she's told her r
that she no longer wants to see me. Did I do anythi
ethical here? I know I had my daughter's best inter
heart.

Answer: So your daughter's blaming you and not her
this, is she?

Stephanie would have a legitimate complaint if y
urged your father to leave her out of his will. She
also have reason to be resentful had you encouraged
leave her the money only on the condition that, for
ple, she complete a college program that you think
fect for her but that she's not interested in.

But you were only looking out for Stephanie wh
did what you did, and there's certainly nothing wron
that. The fact that you urged your father to treat his
daughters differently is in no way unethical. On th
trary, it would have been wrong to make Amanda w
her inheritance just because her sister couldn't be t
with her money yet. And it would have been equally
to have given that much money to someone as immat
Stephanie.

We can't tell you how to get your daughter to sto
ing. But we can tell you to stop worrying that you've
unfair.

you're troubled by what she's doing—and nothing wrong with having a sit-down with your brother, either—you don't have the right to tell her what to do. If these conversations leave you unsatisfied, though, remember that you and your sister can also ask for loans.

My cousins think they're in my mom's will.

When your parent is promising bequests that you know aren't going to happen

Question: I'm an only child, and I know that my mother is leaving her entire estate to me. In fact, she's shown me her will. Unfortunately, sometimes when she has a little too much to drink, Mom likes to hint to her nephews and nieces that she's going to leave them something. For example, I've heard her tell my cousin Laurie that there could be a "nice little sum" in store for her and my cousin Howie that she thinks the painting in her dining room would look good in his house.

Hearing her talk like this makes me very uncomfortable. And I'm worried that when Mom dies, my cousins are going to be angry at me when they don't get anything. What should I do?

Answer: Relax. Unless your mother is saying these things to get special care and attention or the people she's saying them to are planning their lives around her "bequests," don't worry about it.

First of all, you're unlikely to be able to persuade your mother to refrain from this kind of grandstanding. And to go behind her back and tell everyone she's just blowing hot air would be disloyal and make her look foolish. Plus, people do change their wills. It's not inconceivable that your mother could ultimately decide to leave a few things to others in your family.

Most important, though, you probably aren't the only one who's noticed that your mother likes to talk about her "bequests" when she's had a drink or two. Consequently your relatives may be assigning much less weight to these pronouncements than you imagine.

And remember: If upon your mother's death you feel you'd like to make good on her "promises," you are completely free—but by no means obligated—to do so.

✑— HEIR BEWARE —✑

Do many people behave the way the last letter writer's mother does? Apparently so. When we asked the participants in our survey "How common would you say it is for people to deliberately mislead someone into believing they're going to leave that person money when they die?" here's what they told us:

PERCENT WHO SAY

Very common	9%
Somewhat common	37%
Somewhat uncommon	41%
Very uncommon	13%

Source: Fleming & Schwarz survey.

Dad has cut me out of his will.

When a relative is manipulating a parent to get a larger bequest

Question: My sister, Jill, who is extremely devious and emotionally needy, has convinced my elderly father that he should leave all his money to her. Until now, half of Dad's estate was to go to Jill and half to me.

My father's always worried a lot about my sister, and in fact he supported her for a long time until she recently remarried. As our mom used to say, "Jill's a user—sad, but true."

I'm close to Dad, but have never relied on him for money. Jill says that, especially since she has kids and I don't, I don't need the money, and this is the way Dad wants to leave his estate. But I know she just worked on him the way she always has until he gave up and gave in. I understand that it's his money, but would it be wrong for me to speak to my father about this new will?

Answer: Not a bit. The only question is whether you should speak to a lawyer before you speak to your dad or afterward.

What your sister has done—manipulating your father into changing his will—is wrong, and we hope you won't let her get away with it. A lawyer can tell you what your rights are in this situation and how to protect them. And make no mistake about it, you are going to need a lawyer. For no matter how well your talk with your dad goes—no matter what he promises you—you can bet that your sister is going to keep coming after him, preying on his sympathy and hounding the poor man until he once again gives up and gives in.

A lawyer can help you thwart her, and you shouldn't feel bad about involving one. With Jill for a sister, you need all the help you can get.

⌐ BLACK-HEARTED HEIRS ⌐

Just how unusual are people like Jill, the manipulative daughter about whom the writer of the previous letter is so concerned? To find out, we asked the participants in our survey to tell us "How common would you say it is for people to lie, cheat, or pretend to be loving in order to be in someone's will?"

Here are their responses:

PERCENT WHO SAY

Very common	32%
Somewhat common	43%
Somewhat uncommon	22%
Very uncommon	3%

Source: Fleming & Schwarz survey.

It may be of little solace to the letter writer to know that the problems she's experiencing with her sister are far from unique. But what should encourage her is this: The lawyer she tells about Jill's behavior is unlikely to doubt her. On the contrary, she'll be describing a problem he's probably had more than a little experience dealing with.

My father needs a will, and I'm worried that we're unfairly influencing his decisions.

When an elderly parent needs help with estate planning

Question: My brothers and I are trying to help our father draw up his will. The problem is that Dad is quite elderly and having a hard time grasping anything complex. We've brought him with us to speak to the lawyer, but it's not clear he understands all the choices. We want Dad's estate plan to reflect his own wishes, of course. And as future beneficiaries of his estate, we'd also like to minimize estate taxes. Would it be okay for us to present him with just a couple of choices that we think are the best, or must we have the attorney go though every option with him?

Answer: Our bet is that the last thing in the world your father wants to do is sit there while a lawyer explains—or tries to explain—all the possible ways to handle his estate. In fact, we get itchy ourselves just thinking about being in that room.

So here's an honorable alternative: Do your best to determine what your father wants, then have the lawyer present him with a couple of approaches for accomplishing his goals. After all, there is no virtue in presenting him with more choices or more details than he can evaluate or comprehend.

There is nothing unethical about trying to minimize estate taxes, and presenting your father only with estate planning choices that do so is fine—fine provided, first, that those choices also capture what you believe to be his wishes, and second, that you have no reason to believe that he's someone who, for philosophic reasons, believes that trying to minimize taxes is wrong.

The Accidental Bequest

Do most people, as they get older, make an effort to hold on to their money in order to be able to leave a larger amount to their heirs?

In a word, no. Economist Michael Hurd says his research shows that most people both expect to draw down their assets after retirement and in fact actually do so. There's little evidence, he says, that seniors alter the pace at which they spend their money in order to leave a larger estate.

What does shape their planning and spending, though, is a strongly felt need not to run out of money. And since they don't know when they're going to die, seniors tend to hang on to their wealth to guard against ending up resourceless. Consequently, when they do die, there's often more money in their accounts than they otherwise would have chosen—money they were saving for their own use as opposed to saving for their heirs. When this happens, their heirs receive bequests that are larger than the person who died and left them the money intended.

These are what Hurd calls "accidental bequests," and they happen all the time. It's just that most people prefer to think of them as "Mom's generous gift to me" as opposed to the unintended surplus in Mom's rainy day fund.

Chapter Twelve

After the Funeral,
Who Gets What?

Never say you know a man until you have divided
an inheritance with him.

—Johann Kaspar Lavater

A SIXTH-GRADE MATH teacher posed this question to her class:
"A wealthy man dies and leaves ten million dollars. One-
third he leaves to his wife, one-quarter he leaves to his
daughter, one-sixth goes to his nephew, one-eighth goes to
his secretary, and everything else goes to his favorite charity. So, what does each one get?"

Immediately, one of her students raised her hand and
said, "A good lawyer."

There's nothing like the reading of your parents' will
and the divvying up of the treasures in their home to un-

leash rivalries and resentments that have been brewing for decades. Imagine you've been in a turf war with your brother since you were six years old and he stole a piece of your birthday cake. Plus, for the last five years he's been ignoring your pleas to help care for your parents. Now you have to sit down with him and his greedy wife and divide the heirloom silver, the fine china, and the oil painting of your great-grandparents that you want for your children and he wants for his and that most definitely can't be cut in half. . . . Good luck!

✎— JUST FOR OPENERS —✎

One out of two people report having run into trouble with friends or family members over the terms of a relative's will.

and

One out of ten have experienced a lot of trouble on this score.

Source: *Money* survey.

∾

Mom stiffed my sister in her will.
Do I owe her part of my share?

When your mother disinherits someone she shouldn't have

Question: When my mother, an elderly widow, died recently, she left nothing to my sister Susan. Instead, shocking us all, Mom divided her estate evenly between my brother and me. I'm sure she had her reasons for excluding Sue, with whom she'd often locked horns. But I also feel Mom exploited my sister, relying on Sue—not on my brother or me—for considerable care, while never revealing that she'd left Sue out of her will. I want to respect my mother's wishes, and, of course, I'd like to keep my entire inheritance. But I'm wondering, doesn't my sister deserve something?

Answer: Your mother's final wishes *have* been honored: Her estate went to you and your brother. Now it's up to you to remedy the injustice created as a result.

Your letter implies that you and your brother left the responsibility of caring for your mother to your sister, assuming, as did Susan, that your mother was including her in the will. If you and he now fail to share your inheritance with your sister, you'll be stiffing her, just as your mother did.

This is not to say that every child is automatically entitled to an equal portion of a parent's estate. Far from it. But "equality" is not the issue here. The situation you report is one in which your mother routinely called on your sister for assistance while secretly disinheriting her. While undoubtedly was love, not money, that prompted Susan to care for your mother, surely more of the heavy lifting would have fallen to you and your brother had Susan understood that your mother planned to return her devotion with a stab in the back from the grave.

ᦉ— BAD NEWS —ᦇ

How unusual is it for someone to be treated like Susan, the
sister of the writer of the last letter? We asked the participants in the *Money* survey if they had ever been treated unfairly in anyone's will, and here's what the respondents age
fifty-five or older had to say:

PERCENT WHO ANSWERED

Treated unfairly	20%
Never treated unfairly	80%

Source: *Money* survey.

Clearly, being stabbed in the back from the grave is not
such a rare event—one out of five people who've lived long
enough to be likely to have some experience as a beneficiary
say it's happened to them.

I gave Mom the Audubon prints, but my sisters snapped them up after the funeral.

When your siblings want the nice things you gave your parents

Question: I am one of three daughters whose mother recently died. Mom's will was a simple one. It said that everything is to be divided equally among the three of us. This

doesn't seem fair to me. Over the years, I gave my mother many fine things for her home—crystal vases, a Georg Jensen silver tea service, and a pair of Audubon prints, to mention just a few. These weren't birthday or Christmas presents. These were special treats I bought for her, just because I knew she would like them.

While my sisters were always loving daughters, they never gave Mom anything of comparable value—just the usual bedroom slippers or bathrobe-type gifts for her birthday and Christmas. Now they clearly expect to divide all Mom's fine things three ways, even though I paid for almost all of them. Can this be right?

Answer: You can't present a silver tea service to your mother and accept her thanks and gratitude for the gift, then expect to reclaim it upon her death as if it belongs to you and had only been on loan to her.

On the other hand, in being so quick to stake a claim to the treasures that only you gave your mother, your sisters are being at best thoughtless and at worst downright greedy. They certainly owe it to you, first, to acknowledge that you and you alone paid for all those lovely things, and second, to ask you if there aren't at least some of them that you would like to have for yourself. After all, they know that your motive in giving your mother gifts was to make her happy, not to supply them with charming small pieces for their homes.

Had your sisters, like you, been giving your mother expensive gifts over the years, we're sure they'd be more sensitive to the position you're in. Not that giving your mother relatively modest gifts reflects badly on them. But failing to take note that your gifts were significantly more valuable certainly does.

⌒ "WHY DON'T YOU TAKE THE IRONING ⌒ BOARD, AND I'LL TAKE THE EARRINGS."

The woman who wrote the last letter is not alone. Far from it. Close to two-thirds of the participants in the *Money* survey reported having experienced at least some trouble in divvying up a relative's belongings after the person died. Here's how much trouble they've had:

	PERCENT WHO SAID
A lot of trouble	20%
Some trouble	43%
No trouble	37%

Source: *Money* survey.

If you felt so embarrassed by your sister's behavior after your mother died that you couldn't even tell your best friend about it, you can relax. One out of five people have had an equally unpleasant experience—and two more out of the five can probably identify with how you feel.

My friend said she'd leave me $5,000, but I haven't gotten a dime.

When you're promised a bequest and it's not in the will

Question: My college roommate Sharon, who was also my best friend, died of cancer when she was in her thirties. During the last few months of her illness, her mother and I became quite close. And we remained close for about five years afterward, meeting for lunch, exchanging birthday presents, and the like.

Midway through that period, Helen shocked me by saying she planned to leave me $5,000 when she died. I was touched that she thought so much of me, and, of course, thrilled at the prospect of one day receiving such a generous gift.

Three years ago Helen and her husband retired to Florida, and I never saw her again, though we still stayed in touch.

Then, about a year ago, Helen's son called to tell me that Helen had died. A few weeks later, I received a nice note from Helen's husband, thanking me for the condolences I'd sent him. But I have never received my inheritance.

Helen once told me that all of her and her husband's assets were in a so-called "living trust." I know that, while wills are a matter of public record, these trusts are not. So I have no proof that she left me the money. All I can do is ask her husband about it, and he and I were never close.

What should I do?

Answer: Cross your fingers and hope.

There are four possible explanations for why you have

not received the bequest Helen promised you. The first is that Helen wasn't as serious about leaving you the money as she led you to believe. If that's the case, your friend has done you an injustice and, unfortunately, there's not much you can do about it.

A second explanation is that Helen's husband has chosen to ignore his wife's wishes. If you think there's a chance that this is the case, you should consult a lawyer to find out what your options are.

Another, sunnier possibility is that the terms of Helen and her husband's living trust, like most marital trusts, call for the surviving spouse to enjoy all of their money during his or her lifetime and for bequests such as the one you're expecting to be made only after both the husband and wife are gone. For example, Helen's son may not have inherited any money from his mother either. Instead, his inheritance is likely to come when his father dies. And perhaps yours will as well.

The final explanation for your not receiving a bequest is this: At some point after she moved away, Helen and her husband revised the list of beneficiaries of their trust, and you were not included in the new list. While this may seem unfair, you have to remember that wills and living trusts are not chiseled in stone. They're a snapshot of how a person feels at a particular moment in time. And feelings change. Favorite charities can become more important, an adult child can develop a special need, and out-of-town friends can, over time, come to seem less important than they were when they were a regular and significant part of the person's life.

So what should you do? If you think there's a chance that Helen's husband essentially stole (by refusing to distribute) a bequest you are certain she wanted you to have upon her death, see a lawyer. But if not, we see no merit in questioning Helen's husband, who could mistake your understandable curiosity for unbecoming greed. Instead, we suggest, as we said at the outset, that you cross your fingers and hope—hope that you remain among the beneficiaries of Helen's and her husband's trust.

⌒ **ARE BEQUESTS ETCHED IN STONE?** ⌒

Imagine that—as happened to the woman who wrote the previous letter—someone promises you a bequest. Is this a promise the person is obligated to keep, no matter how many years go by after the promise is made?

That's a question we put to half the participants in our survey, and 20 percent—one in five—said yes, the person is obligated to keep the promise.

The other half of the participants were asked to put themselves in the position of the person making the promise. Of them we asked, once you promise to leave someone money in your will, do you have an obligation to do so, no matter how many years go by after the promise is made?

To this question, 41 percent—or roughly two in five respondents—said yes, they'd be obligated to keep the promise.

So there you have it. Would-be benefactors appear to take their promises significantly more seriously than do their prospective heirs. But that said, the majority in each camp believes promises such as the one made to the writer of the last letter are not lifetime obligations.

Which is not to say that there aren't a lot of disappointed people when the would-be benefactors change their minds and change their wills.

Source: Fleming & Schwarz survey.

⌒— **COMING UP EMPTY** —⌒

One out of eight people say they expected to
inherit money or something of value from someone
who, when he or she died, ended up leaving
them nothing.

Source: Fleming & Schwarz survey.

Who gets Grandma's jewelry?

When one relative lays claim to all the good stuff

Question: When my grandmother died last year, she divided
her money equally among my mother, my aunt, and my
uncle. Grandma had several nice pieces of jewelry, none of
which was mentioned in the will. My Aunt Sherry claims
that Grandma often told her she wanted these pieces—two
antique Navajo bracelets and a pair of sapphire earrings—
to go to Sherry's daughter Brianne "because they had the
same coloring and the same sign." But my mom and I
never heard Grandma say anything like that, and this
wouldn't be the first time that Aunt Sherry lied about stuff
like this.

So when Mom found the jewelry when she was cleaning out Grandma's things, she gave one of the bracelets to
me, one to my Uncle David's daughter Greta, and the earrings to Brianne. My aunt is furious. Do you think Mom
did anything wrong?

Answer: As a matter of fact, yes.

Just because your grandmother's will doesn't specifically mention her jewelry doesn't mean the jewelry is up for grabs. Almost certainly her will entrusts someone with the responsibility for distributing her personal property. And if your mother isn't that person, she was wrong to take it upon herself to divvy up the bracelets and earrings.

Just because Aunt Sherry's claim seems implausible (and we share your skepticism), it doesn't mean your mother was free to dismiss it out of hand and make up her own rules for who should get what. Rather, your aunt should have been given the chance to back up her assertion that the jewelry had been promised to her daughter.

Even if she couldn't, she still had a right to expect a less arbitrary distribution of her mother's jewelry. For example: Each heir could have been offered the opportunity to select one piece of jewelry, with the order of selection determined by cutting cards, drawing straws, or the like.

A luck-of-the-draw process may not be perfect, but it is fair. And it puts a stop to the shenanigans of the folks who think everything nice has their name on it just as effectively as your mother's high-handed approach did.

ᦡ— **THERE'S ONE IN EVERY FAMILY** —ᦡ

Seven out of eight people agree that—when a family goes to
divvy up the belongings of a relative who's died—there's
always one person who tries to get more than his or her share.

Source: *Money* survey.

Blue Is for Brittany, Green Is for Greg

Our neighbor Pauline is a widow in her eighties. Visit her
home, and you'll find a small tag stuck to the back or bottom of every item of value there. The tags are in different
colors, and each color corresponds to one of Pauline's children, grandchildren, nephews, and nieces. When Pauline
dies, each of her heirs is to receive the furnishings marked
with his or her color.

Pauline says she can't imagine letting her family divvy
up her things on their own. Some of them, she knows, are
pretty pushy, and she can't bear the thought of her death
setting off a squabble over her treasures. Besides, she enjoys showing the members of her family the objects she is
leaving them and explaining to them what the items represent.

Pauline is no fool. She knows that some of her things
will end up on eBay. But she also takes great pleasure in
knowing that the items she treasures most will be going to
the people she wants to have them and that her passing will
not trigger a battle royal among her heirs.

Not everyone cares as much as Pauline does about who gets what when they're gone. And not everyone has her patience. But we all would do well to take note of what she has done, namely: spelled things out in a way that spares her loved ones the difficult and often resentment-engendering task of divvying up her valuables.

Our advice: You don't need to put a tag on everything you own. But if you have a will, you really ought to put a letter in with it telling your executor who you'd like to see get (1) those things you treasure most and (2) those things that others are most likely to covet.

Chapter Thirteen

Neighbors from Hell
(and Other Places)

⌘

The Bible tells us to love our neighbors, and also to
love our enemies; probably because generally they
are the same people.

—G. K. Chesterton

FRIENDS WHO LIVE in Alaska told us this story: There's a particularly tasty berry that grows in the rural part of the state
where they live, and a nice patch of these berries grows almost directly under their kitchen window. Over the course
of the long winter, they periodically gaze out at the berry
patch and happily contemplate the summer months when
they'll be enjoying the fruit.

A couple of springs ago when they looked out their
window, what did they see but a goat grazing his way
through their almost-ripe berries. Our friends recognized

the goat as belonging to their nearest neighbor, so they walked him the mile or so back to the neighbor's house and asked the neighbor to please keep the goat away from their berries. "Sorry," the neighbor said, "but we don't like to tie him up, and we can't help it if he likes berries."

"But they're our berries," our friends said. "They're on our property. So please see that your goat doesn't eat them."

Our friends might as well have been speaking to the goat. The neighbors, instead of tethering their animal, allowed it to return every spring until our friends went to the considerable expense of building a fence around their berry patch—a fence to protect them from the behavior of an inconsiderate neighbor who lived more than a mile away.

This story has two morals. First, when you have truly terrible neighbors, distance alone is no protection. You need fences—and maybe walls and moats as well. Second, once you realize you have bad neighbors—when they reveal that they are utterly unconcerned about the consequences of their behavior for you—build the fence immediately. Don't wait for common decency to enter into their thinking, because it's not going to happen. Worry instead that they're going to get a second goat.

∽

What can we do about the slobs next door?

When your neighbors' property looks like a pigsty

Question: We're about to put our large, well-maintained home on the market. Unfortunately, our next-door neighbors' place is a pigsty. Just to give you some idea of how bad it is, a boat with a broken-down clothes dryer in it has been sitting in the middle of their yard for the past six months, and a car with two wheels missing fills half their driveway. My wife and I are wondering, are we within our rights to insist they clean up this mess? We're afraid the condition of their home will affect the price we get for ours.

Answer: Private property is a wonderful thing. Barring restrictive community ordinances and rules set by home-owner associations (and since you don't mention them, we assume they don't apply here), you have the freedom to put anything you like in your front yard. And so do your neighbors. As inconsiderate as beaching a boat there may be— and your neighbors do indeed sound like pigs—they're under no obligation to modify the way they live in order to maximize the price you'll get for your home.

Fortunately you have three approaches at your disposal besides invoking a right you only wish you had. First, you can appeal to your neighbors' sense of civility: Ask them (nicely, of course) to clean up their place as a courtesy to you. Or you can appeal to their economic self-interest: The more your house sells for, after all, the more their house is likely to sell for when that day comes. And finally, you can offer to pay them to make their property look more presentable.

Let's say you're successful, and we hope you are. Don't forget you have a moral, and possibly legal, obligation to disclose to prospective buyers the usual condition of the house next door. It's okay, of course, to spruce things up when you go to sell your home, but not to sweep price-affecting problems under the rug.

Our neighbor says she can't afford an increase in the homeowners' fees.

When you live in a condo

Question: My wife and I live in a six-unit condo complex in California. There's no outside management here. Instead, the homeowners get together monthly and agree on what needs to be done. At a recent meeting, we decided we needed more earthquake insurance. To pay for it, we'll have to increase our homeowners' fees by eighty-five dollars a month. The problem is, one of the homeowners, a nice widow, says she's on a fixed income and can't afford the increase. We don't want to be callous about our friend and neighbor's plight, but we also don't want to be without this insurance. Ethically, is it wrong to get the insurance and increase our fees?

Answer: Like you, we have considerable sympathy for widows with limited resources. But we are much less sympathetic toward people who think their problems are automatically your problems. The fact is, condominiums, like single-family houses, need to be adequately insured and maintained. If your fellow owner can't afford to pay her share of these basic expenses, then she is living in a home she can't afford, and she needs to move—unless, of course, the remaining homeowners are willing to subsidize her every time a new expense arises.

To be sure, the world is a better place when condo owners try to accommodate each other's needs. But what your fellow owner wants is not that you, say, postpone upgrading the landscaping while she gets her finances in order. Rather, she wants you to either permanently pay her share of the earthquake insurance or take the risk associated with being underinsured.

Her financial situation doesn't excuse a position so unfair to her fellow owners.

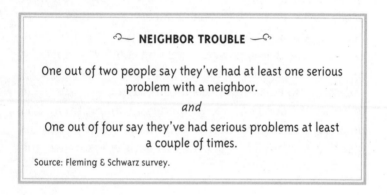

⌒— **NEIGHBOR TROUBLE** —⌒

One out of two people say they've had at least one serious problem with a neighbor.

and

One out of four say they've had serious problems at least a couple of times.

Source: Fleming & Schwarz survey.

Should we lie so our friends' daughter can stay in the local high school?

When a neighbor asks you to do something underhanded

Question: Our next-door neighbors, with whom we've been friends for years, suffered a big financial setback. As a result, they've been forced to sell their home and move to a less expensive community nearby—a town whose schools are pretty mediocre. Recently they asked us to allow their fourteen-year-old daughter to list our address as her residence so that she can continue to attend the top-rated schools where we live. What should we do?

Answer: Just say no.

As much as you might like to lend a hand, your obligation to help your friends ends at the point at which they ask for assistance that shortchanges others. And that's exactly what they want you to do when they ask you to sneak their child into a school that your neighbors are paying for and they aren't.

Of course there's always room for one more student in a school. But there isn't room for *every* child who would like to go to school in a district as good as yours. A line has to be drawn somewhere, and there's nothing unfair or unreasonable about drawing it between the kids of parents who pay taxes to support the schools and the kids of parents who don't.

On another front, think about the lesson you and your friends would be teaching their daughter: that adversity justifies cheating. Yeah, yeah. We know. It's rule-bending, not cheating. But call it what you will, it's encouraging a fourteen-year-old girl to use a false address to get something she's not entitled to—something others paid for and her family didn't. That's a lesson in lying—a lesson that shouldn't be taught.

Neighborhood Watch

Imagine yourself in this situation: You have a neighbor who leaves his beaten-up motor home parked in front of your house for weeks—and sometimes months—at a time. When you asked him to move it, he got angry, told you "You can't tell *me* where to park," and hasn't spoken to you since.

Now your neighbor is away on vacation, and you can see that his irrigation system has broken and his yard is beginning to flood. Your property is uphill from his, so you are in no danger. But if the irrigation system isn't turned off, his yard will be under water and his basement will flood. What would you be most likely to do?

- Do nothing and let the water flow.

- Give the flooding time to do some damage, then contact your neighbor's sister, who lives nearby and who probably knows how to reach him.

- Contact his sister right away.

- Contact his sister right away, then see if you can find a way to turn off the water from outside his house.

- Instead of either trying to help or doing nothing, throw detergent or red dye in the water.

When we asked this question in the *Money* survey, roughly three-quarters of the respondents said they would contact the sister right away, and two-thirds of those three-quarters said they'd also try to turn the water off themselves. Good for them.

On the other hand, roughly one in four people said

they'd either sit tight and do nothing at all, or contact the neighbor's sister only after the flooding had had time to do some damage. You won't catch us condemning these folks. While common courtesy would normally dictate that they promptly call the sister, the neighbor's behavior has taken common courtesy off the table.

If the neighbor needed help in a medical emergency, of course they should come to his aid. And if he complained about their barking dog, they should be responsive. But their obligation to be a good neighbor to a particularly bad one ends well short of being obliged to look out for his property when he's out of town.

And what about throwing detergent or red dye in the water? While of course that's unethical, we'll admit to admiring the spirit of the few survey respondents—under 1 percent—who said they'd do it. If nothing else, these folks understand what it takes to get the attention of a selfish and completely inconsiderate neighbor.

We're sick of paying for other people's kids.

When neighbors stick you with their kids' tab

Question: We have many children, and our children have many friends. Often their friends are visitors in our home, and it's not unusual for one or more of them to wind up coming along when our family goes out to a movie, the skating rink, or a casual meal. Are we wrong to expect these kids' parents to chip in for such excursions? Just with the snacks, this is getting very expensive.

Answer: If you invite—however indirectly or reluctantly—one of your children's friends to join you in a family activity, the child is your guest and shouldn't be expected to pay. That doesn't mean the child's parents have no responsibility, though. On the contrary, if you're picking up the tab with any regularity, they have an obligation to reciprocate your hospitality and generosity, or to insist that their child pay his own way.

Parents also have an obligation to teach their children that, while accepting a small treat or two from their hosts is fine, asking at the movies for a large popcorn, a candy bar, and a soda isn't. "Show consideration for other people's pocketbooks" may not rank with "Always tell the truth" as a guiding principle, but no one should pass puberty without having grasped it.

All of this said, there may be a simpler solution to your immediate problem than counting on your kids' friends' parents to do the right thing. Remember: It's perfectly okay to send a visiting child home when your family decides to go out. So should the expense start to outweigh the pleasure of your children's friends' company, stop inviting them to come along.

My accountant will hate me for sending my neighbor to him.

When someone who's trouble wants a referral

Question: My neighbor Mark recently fired his accountant. Remembering that I've spoken well of my accountant in the past, Mark has asked for his name. Must I give it to him?

Mark is a good guy, but in my opinion, he can be overly aggressive in his personal business dealings. In particular, he always seems to be challenging bills, threatening not to pay them, and renegotiating prices.

I want to help Mark, but I don't want my good relationship with my very good accountant to be soured by the way in which Mark is sure to treat him. Am I ethically obligated to give Mark my accountant's name and number?

Answer: Ethics don't require that you help every person who could use a hand. A drowning man, a lost child, a flu-stricken friend? Of course you should help. But a neighbor in need of an accountant? There you have some slack.

Especially if you feel that Mark is going to poison a relationship you value, you are under no obligation to give him your accountant's name.

And how should you go about saying no? By telling your neighbor the truth in the nicest possible way. You won't enjoy the conversation, but it's the price you must pay for the temporary insanity that led you to tell Mark about your accountant in the first place.

⟋⟋ HONEY, DON'T ANSWER THE DOOR! ⟍⟍

Just how willing are people to allow their neighbors to impose on them? We thought we'd find out by asking the participants in our survey how they would respond to their neighbors asking for an arguably unreasonable favor. Here's the question we asked and the responses we received:

"Imagine that you have a cordial relationship with your next-door neighbors, but that you're not really friends. How would you respond if they knocked on your door and asked for each of the following favors:"

	PERCENT OF SURVEY RESPONDENTS WHO SAID THEY WOULD SAY:		
FAVOR	YES	YES, BUT THE REQUEST IS UNREASONABLE	NO
They ask if you could give their cat its medication twice a day while they go away for the weekend.	65%	5%	30%
They ask if they can use your bathroom for a day or two while their sewage line is being repaired.	56%	15%	29%
They ask you to remove a small tree from your yard because one of them is allergic to it.	34%	10%	56%

(continued)

bought by a young family who tore out and replaced the landscaping. In the process, they put in a stepping-stone path from the sidewalk to their backyard—a path that, for the first ten feet, runs across our property. The stepping-stones are not particularly conspicuous, and they look very nice. But they also make it appear as if a portion of our front yard goes with our neighbors' home, and this, in turn, makes our property look smaller than it actually is.

When we spoke to our neighbors about this, they said they'd be happy to sign any document we want acknowledging that a portion of their path is on our lot. Beyond that, though, they acted as if we were accusing them of trying to steal our property. And when we assured them we weren't, they kept saying, "So what's the problem?"

My husband thinks we should just let the whole thing go in the interest of harmony. But I think we should insist they remove those stones that are on our property. Why should the appearance of our home suffer because asking the neighbors to remove them will hurt their feelings?

What do you think?

Answer: We think your neighbors have done something wrong—and inexcusable—and you should ask them to remedy it. And, if they don't, you should remove the stones yourselves.

If their property looks larger (and presumably nicer) and your property looks smaller (and presumably less attractive) as the result of those stones, they *have* stolen your property. The fact that you own the land is just a technical-

They ask you to keep your young children inside on Saturday mornings until ten, because they like to sleep late.	18%	4%
They ask you if their parents can stay with you for a night or two until the new sofa bed they've ordered arrives.	10%	6%

Source: Fleming & Schwarz survey.

Clearly there are a lot of kind-hearted people out ther so kind-hearted they're often willing to bear considera imposition. But what the survey results also reveal is how luctant many folks are to risk giving offense to the peop with whom they share walls or property lines. How can y tell? Look carefully at the two columns of Yes answers, ar you'll see that in four of the five scenarios, over 20 percent the people who said yes also said that they did so believin that the request was unreasonable.

Our neighbors put a stepping-stone path across our lawn.

When a neighbor infringes on your property line

Question: Our home is on a cul-de-sac, which means ou lot, like those of our immediate neighbors, is oddl shaped—relatively narrow in front by the street, but mucl wider in the rear. Recently, the house next to ours wa:

ity when they've taken from you the benefit the piece of land provides.

The sad truth is, there are people in this world who are "takers." Pretending their actions cost others nothing, takers help themselves to what isn't theirs. They take seats for their coats in crowded movie theaters, they park their cars without regard to how many spaces they use, and they store their bicycles and baby strollers in the common areas of apartment buildings and condominiums.

That's to name but a few of their sins. The list is endless.

Takers are emboldened to behave the way they do because they know it's a pretty good bet that most people would prefer to avoid a confrontation rather than to call them on their actions. Your neighbors, with their disingenuous "So what's the problem" routine, are counting on you and your husband to worry more about hurting their feelings and maintaining harmony than about the appearance of your home. You shouldn't let them get away with it.

Push back—establish a boundary, for their property and for their behavior—and eventually your neighbors will realize that you are not going to allow yourselves to be taken advantage of. But accommodate them on the stones, and, next thing you know, you'll find their badminton net stretched across a portion of your front lawn, their kids skateboarding in your driveway, and the last two feet of their new toolshed extending into your backyard.

Chapter Fourteen

You Did *What* to My Car?

Lending is for the lucky and the brave.
—Fortune cookie saying

A FRIEND TOLD us this story: Her boyfriend, Ben, took four months off from work not long ago and went to Chile to surf. While he was there, his buddy Mike came to visit, and one day when the surf was particularly powerful, Mike asked if he could borrow Ben's special, heavy board—a board made for that type of surf. Ben hated to lend anyone his good board. But realizing that Mike had traveled thousands of miles to get to these waves, he said okay.

And, of course, Mike cracked the board. While he immediately assured Ben that he'd pay the $150 or so it would cost to repair the crack, Ben knew that once a board cracks, it's never quite the same no matter how good the repair. So, reluctantly, he told Mike that he felt Mike owed him a new board, not a repaired one. Mike didn't disagree. But as he told Ben, he'd spent all of his money on the trip to Chile, and he didn't have anywhere near the $800 it would cost to replace Ben's board.

Since Ben had sunk just about all of his savings into his surfing sabbatical, he, too, was in no position to spend $800 on a new board. So for the remainder of this once-in-a-lifetime trip to some of the most exhilarating surf in the world, one of Ben's best boards had become one of his worst. . . . End of story.

Our point? If you think that property-related money-and-ethics problems are confined to the materialistic, think again. Not even living the carefree life of a surfer in Chile spares you from the problems that can arise when a friend or relative wants to borrow something of yours. Neither does lending your belongings only to honorable people ensure a happy ending when they do.

~

My friend's two-year-old broke our $500 vase,
and she hasn't offered to replace it.

When someone's child is destructive

Question: Last year I took my son Dylan over to my friend Kristin's for a play date and, while we weren't looking, Dylan knocked over and broke a terra-cotta urn. I offered to pay for it, but Kristin said "Don't be silly. Boys will be boys, and these kinds of things happen." Since I knew the urn came from Pottery Barn and cost around fifty bucks—in other words, it wasn't an heirloom, and it wasn't particularly expensive—I apologized for my son's behavior and let it go.

Last week Kristin dropped by, bringing along her two-year-old, Madison. Madison's at a bad stage right now, and had I known they were coming, I would have put a few things away. But I didn't have a chance to, and five minutes after they arrived, Madison knocked a Waterford vase onto the kitchen floor, where it shattered. Kristin, of course, helped me clean up the broken glass and told me how sorry she was about what Madison had done. But she made no offer to pay for the vase.

I realize that when Dylan broke that urn in her home, Kristin didn't want or expect me to pay for it. But this is different. The vase Madison broke was really valuable. It was a wedding gift from my favorite aunt, and it cost over $500. Shouldn't Kristin be paying to replace it?

Answer: Kristin most certainly should be offering to pay for or replace the vase her daughter broke, just as you should have insisted on paying for or replacing the urn your son broke in her home. After all, a fifty-dollar home furnishing is not a toy or a crayon—not, that is, an object all parents understand can get broken when children play.

But since you didn't run over to Pottery Barn and replace the urn as you should have—since, instead, you bought into Kristin's "boys will be boys" rule—you're now obligated to live with its corollary, namely: "Madison will be Madison."

Why should I have to pay to replace his old muffler?

When something borrowed accidentally breaks

Question: When the clutch failed on my station wagon the night before I was to drive my sons to a soccer tournament, my neighbor lent me his SUV for the day. Unfortunately, on the way home from the tournament, the muffler fell off. So I took his car to a muffler shop, where they told me that what happened was in all likelihood the result of long-term wear and tear and not anything I did. Under these circumstances, am I obligated to pay for the new muffler?

Answer: In general, when you borrow something, you're obligated to return it in the condition in which it was lent to you. The fact that accidents happen doesn't get you off the hook. So, for example, had a tree fallen on your neighbor's SUV while it was parked at the soccer tournament, you would have been obligated to pay for any repairs not covered by insurance. The point is, you don't get to enjoy the use of something for free while the owner bears the risk of whatever befalls it while it's in your possession.

On the other hand, what borrowers are not obligated to do is contribute to the long-term maintenance of something they borrow briefly and infrequently. While the muffler problem appears to fall into this category, we gather from what you say that there is no way of knowing for sure that a worn but still functioning muffler wasn't done in by, say, a rock you drove over or a rut in the road. Understand we believe that you *probably* weren't responsible for the muffler falling off. But in this situation, the benefit of the doubt goes to the lender, who was kind enough to let you use his car and expected nothing in return except that the car be returned in the same condition as it was when you borrowed it.

⌒ **ARE ALL BORROWERS CREATED EQUAL?** ⌒

How inclined are most folks to do what we encouraged the last letter writer to do, namely: accept full responsibility for anything that goes wrong with something they've borrowed? To find out, we asked the participants in the *Money* survey how they would respond in the following situation:

Imagine that you've borrowed a neighbor's power mower—something you frequently do, and he doesn't seem to mind. While you're mowing your lawn, it dies on you. What would you be most likely to do?

Here are their responses:

PERCENT WHO ANSWERED

Offer to pay to have it repaired.	53%
Offer to split the cost of repairing it with your neighbor.	25%
Offer to pay at least something toward the repair.	21%
Return it to him as is—after all, it's not a new lawn mower.	1%

Source: *Money* survey.

(*continued*)

The good news here is that about half the people are willing to step up and do the right thing. And another quarter apparently want to be fair, though they fail to see the unfairness in borrowing something—regularly, no less—and not assuming the risk for it while it's in their care. On the other hand, a final quarter, or thereabouts, appear to be cheapskates—folks whose first instinct is to pay as little as possible, or even nothing.

My sister acts like I'm a thief.

When your sister wants her things back for no reason

Question: Rosemary, my oldest sister, stopped entertaining after her husband died and she moved into a small apartment. But she kept all of her good silverware and serving pieces. Occasionally I borrow some of these things when my husband and I give a party. While I've returned everything she's ever lent me, I sometimes hang on to a few pieces for a while because I know she doesn't entertain anymore, and we frequently have a use for them.

Recently Rosemary has started asking for everything back as soon as I finish with it. She's not senile, and I know she doesn't think I'm stealing from her. But still, this feels like a slap in the face. Is it?

Answer: Think of it more as a wake-up call.

As we understand it, you've been asking to borrow your

sister's silver for a specific event, then treating what she's lent you as if it were on permanent loan. In addition, you seem to have unilaterally decided that you need her silver more than she does, even though that's not your decision to make. In short, you've begun to treat your sister's things as if they were your own. While we know you're not stealing Rosemary's silver, we can see why your behavior could lead her—and her children—to worry that you believe you have a claim on what isn't yours.

When people lend you something, you have an obligation to return it when they'd like it back, not when you think they need it. Whether or not they plan to use it is irrelevant. It's their property, not yours; they've done you a favor by letting you borrow it; and they don't need a reason for wanting it back. Indeed, it's wrong to make them ask you to return it. No one likes to do that, and you should have spared your sister that awkwardness. She undoubtedly feels as uncomfortable as you do, and *she's* done nothing wrong.

ᖯ— **"NEVER LEND ANYTHING TO RACHEL."** —ᖰ

Three out of four people agree that in most families, there's always somebody who borrows things and never returns them.

Source: Fleming & Schwarz survey.

My friend took advantage of my honorable behavior.

When you reimburse a friend for an item you've
borrowed and lost, is it wrong for your friend to spend
the money on something else?

Question: When I borrowed my friend Kate's bicycle to go
to the library, I forgot to lock it up, and the bike was stolen.
Kate told me the bike—which was only two weeks old—had
cost $1,200, an amount I promptly PayPaled her. At Kate's
the other day, though, I noticed that the bike she'd bought
to replace the one I'd lost was obviously a cheaper model.
She explained she'd decided to spend $800 on the bike and
use the rest of the money for an iPod docking station.
Shouldn't she have spent the entire $1,200 on a bike, since
that's what she asked for? We're both junior faculty, and I
would love to have kept that $400 myself if Kate didn't
need it to replace the lost bike.

Answer: We feel your pain. The fact is, though, that the ethical obligation in this situation runs only one way: from you,
who lost the bike, to Kate, the friend who lent it to you.
While it would have been very nice of Kate to settle for the
$800 her new bike cost instead of the $1,200 the stolen bike
was worth, accepting your $1,200 wasn't wrong. After all,
she had just written a check for $1,200 herself. Kate was
insensitive, though, and less concerned about your pocket-
book than you might have hoped, given your relationship. A
better friend would have given $400 back to you and said
she realized she was satisfied with a less expensive bike.

To put it another way, being ethical and being a good friend are not necessarily the same thing. Ethically speaking, Kate did nothing wrong. But as your friend, she blew it.

⁀ HER BABYSITTER STOLE MY RING. ⁀

Imagine that you're visiting a friend and you take your expensive ring off while you help in the kitchen. When you go to put it on again, you discover the ring is gone. You later learn that your friend's babysitter stole it and sold it on eBay, along with some of your friend's jewelry. Assuming that your friend is not insured for this kind of theft and neither are you, should your friend reimburse you for your ring?

That's a question we put to the participants in our survey, and here are their answers:

PERCENT WHO SAY

Yes, pay whatever the ring cost.	12%
Yes, pay some portion of the cost of the ring.	11%
No.	77%

Source: Fleming & Schwarz survey.

In other words, over three out of four people believe the host bears no responsibility. Unfortunately they're wrong.

Individuals have an ethical, and often legal, obligation to provide for the safety and well-being of the friends they

(continued)

invite into their homes. Step through a rotting board, and your hosts are responsible for whatever injuries you incur, regardless of whether they knew the board was unsound. In a similar vein, the homeowner in this scenario is responsible for the behavior of her employee, even if she had no reason to think the babysitter was dishonest. Ignorance and a pure heart don't wash away responsibility. She owes her visitor a new ring.

Still, the ring owner—like Kate, the owner of the bicycle in the previous letter—might want to keep in mind that the homeowner is her friend, not her insurance company. So when the homeowner offers to pay for that nice new ring, her friend—as a friend—should consider picking up half the tab herself.

I'm sick of Angela borrowing my car.

When a friend borrows something all the time

Question: I am very close with my next-door neighbor Angela, and we've always borrowed things—big and small—from one another without any problems. But this summer Angela's son has gotten a job that he needs to drive to, leaving their family one car short. So Angela's been borrowing my car now and then, and here's the problem: She'll ask me if she can use it to visit her mother, for example, and while she is happy to go whatever day I say the car's available, I still have to plan to be without a car for a day. Angela always fills the gas tank after she uses it, but this just means

I have to get some gas before she borrows it, because I don't want to stick her with an expensive fill-up. More important, I don't want the gas. I want the freedom not to have to plan things around Angela. Am I being selfish here, or am I right to feel that Angela is asking for too much?

Answer: You're right. . . . And you're not being selfish.

Given your friendship, it would not be unreasonable for Angela to ask to borrow your car in a pinch. But she's not in a pinch. She's facing a summer-long car shortage. That's a problem for which she needs to find a solution, not a friend to share it with.

And let's be frank: Angela has some other options besides your car. For one, she could drive her son to and from work on the days she needs a car. This may be inconvenient for one or both of them, but that's no reason why you should be inconvenienced instead.

Alternately, Angela could take taxis or rent a car now and then. Just because these options can be expensive doesn't mean you should make sacrifices in order for her to save a buck—not for an entire summer.

No doubt Angela has heard of taxis and rental cars, but apparently she believes that friends don't let friends use them. So unless, fortified with the knowledge that we're on your side, you feel comfortable saying no to Angela, you're going to have to wait for her son's job to end. When it does, we hope she realizes how much she's imposed on you and sends you a small truckload of fine chocolates, luxury bath products, or whatever else you love. It's the least she can do.

Making People Whole
WHEN BORROWED ITEMS ARE LOST OR BROKEN

"I hate to tell you this, but you know that camera you lent me?"

There's a fundamental rule that applies when people borrow something from you and then break it or lose it: They have to make you whole. Making you whole doesn't mean finding almost all of the pieces and gluing the vase back together. It doesn't mean getting the candle wax out of a tablecloth to the best of their ability. Making you, the lender, whole means making certain you're no worse off for having lent them something. For example:

A friend borrows your sweater and spills red wine all over it, ruining it. The sweater was three years old, in good condition, and still in style. What should your friend do?

The answer lies not in figuring out the dollar value of the lost or damaged item, but in assessing its value to you. In the case at hand, you lost a perfectly good sweater, so that's what the borrower needs to buy you—a new sweater of comparable quality to the one that was ruined.

It makes no difference that you have already gotten three years of wear out of the sweater or that an insurance company might say that a sweater costing one hundred dollars three years ago is worth only thirty dollars today. You lost a good sweater, and thirty dollars isn't going to replace it.

If, however, you were about to donate that sweater to Goodwill, you should tell your friend not to worry about replacing it. But, even then, your friend should still take you out to a nice lunch.

What if friends damage or destroy an item that is terribly expensive?

Too bad for them.

There's no reason why you, having been kind enough to lend them something quite valuable, should not be made whole just because making you whole is going to cost them real money.

What if the item they borrowed is irreplaceable?

Say friends break an antique platter that you lent them, a platter that's been in your family for many generations.

Your friends should insist you pick out a lovely new platter or something else quite fine that appeals to you, buy it for you, and tell you they hope that, in time, it too will become a family treasure. And because the platter they broke was irreplaceable, they should err on the side of spending too much.

What if the item is in worse condition for their having borrowed it, but still usable?

Say friends borrow your Cuisinart food processor and burn out the motor. They have it repaired, and now, while the Cuisinart runs again, it doesn't run as well as it did when you lent it to them.

Ethics dictates that your friends buy you a new Cuisinart. Common sense adds that they should hang on to your
old one, so they never need to borrow yours again.

*What if the item they borrowed was lost or damaged through
no fault of theirs?*

Say burglars broke into your friends' home and stole the
GPS navigator they'd borrowed from you, along with a lot
of their electronic equipment.

   Either they or their insurance company need to pay for
your GPS (and if they're insured, but their insurance company doesn't pay one hundred cents on the dollar, they need
to make up the difference). When friends or relatives borrow an item, they're responsible for what happens to it. Period. The fact that a borrower is not to blame for the loss of
the item has nothing to do with the situation. As we pointed
out earlier, borrowers can't expect to enjoy the use of something for free while the owner bears the risk of whatever
befalls it while it's in their possession.

"Unfortunately, I won't be able to lend this to you."

While borrowers are obligated to make their friends whole
for items they have on loan that they lose or damage, lenders have a few obligations as well. Here they are:

1. If someone asks to borrow something that is particularly
   valuable, be certain he or she understands its value.
For example, if a friend asks to borrow a pair of expensive

earrings, be certain she doesn't mistake them for costume jewelry and treat them accordingly. You don't want your friendship to be rattled by a situation in which, only after losing an earring, does your friend learn that the pair cost $750 and not the $75 she imagined.

2. If someone careless asks to borrow something that is particularly valuable, don't lend it.

Your brother may be angry with you if you fail to lend him your car while his is in the shop. But his anger pales in comparison to the resentment you'll feel when, instead of returning your car, he gives you the phone number of his insurance agent and the address of the body shop to which your car has been towed.

3. If someone asks to borrow something that you would absolutely hate to lose, don't lend it.

We all have a favorite sweater or vase or tie or tool. Don't risk upsetting a friendship by lending it. No matter how careful your friend may be, children still knock things over, dogs mistake clothes for toys, and lightning strikes. When something along this line happens, you're going to be very angry at the borrower—angrier than you have a right to be.

4. If a close friend or relative loses something of yours, you shouldn't insist on being made whole if you'd be just as happy with something less expensive—or with nothing at all.

Imagine you bought an expensive digital camera that you've come to realize has more features than you could ever hope to master. A good friend who is planning to get a new camera asks to give yours a try, and while it's in his possession, his two-year-old throws it into a koi pond. Clearly your friend is obligated to replace the camera or to write you a check for what it cost. But if your old camera cost $500, and you're planning to replace it with a $250 camera, $250 is all you should ask your friend for.

Does the same apply if the child of someone you barely know gets hold of your camera and ruins it? No. You don't owe an acquaintance the same consideration as you do a close friend or relative.

5. When you have considerably more resources than the person who is obligated to make you whole, consider—as an act of friendship or an act of charity—forgiving the debt.

That's not to say that just because you make more than your cousin who borrowed and ruined your new lightweight tent, you should automatically tell him to forget about it. But if someone—especially someone you're close to—has lost or damaged something expensive of yours and you can either easily live without it or afford to replace it much more easily than the borrower can, you should discourage the borrower from going into a hole to make you whole.

Which brings us to the final commandment in the lender's bible:

6. Don't lend something to someone who can't afford to replace it—not unless you are fully prepared to say, should it be lost or damaged, "Don't worry about it."

Chapter Fifteen

Let's Break a Deal

―――――――――――――― ⟨⟩ ――――――――――――――

Know each other as if you were brothers; negotiate
deals with each other as if you were strangers.
—Arabian proverb

Your sister asks you for $600 so she can take the computer
classes that she says will make it easier for her to find work.
You write the check. But later you learn that she spent the
money on clothes because the classes filled up before she
got around to enrolling and because, she says, she "needed
new clothes for job interviews anyhow."

You sign on to take your fifteen-year-old son and three of
his classmates away for a ski weekend. The deal is that
you'll rent the cabin and buy the groceries and that, when
you return, the other parents will reimburse you for their
kids' shares of these expenses. Before you finalize the ar-

rangements, you tell all the parents that the rent on the cabin is about to become nonrefundable, and everyone says fine. Then, the day before you leave, one of the boys has an asthma attack, and his parents decide to keep him home. They also decide that, since the incident was unforeseeable, they have no obligation to pay their share of the rent on the cabin.

Your mother, who lives in a small apartment not far from your home, has reached an age where she needs considerable care and attention. So you and your sister, who lives across the country, make a deal: You'll look after Mom nine months of the year, and your sister will take her in June, July, and August. But last year, your mother spent only six weeks with your sister because your brother-in-law chose June to have his knee replacement surgery. And this year your sister tells you that she and her husband would like to celebrate their twenty-fifth wedding anniversary by spending August in Italy, where their daughter is a student.

FOR SOME PEOPLE, a deal is a deal only for as long as it remains convenient to honor it. As soon as their personal needs conflict with the terms of the arrangement, the deal is off. The discouraging thing is that we're not talking about cynical people here—not those Kim Jong Ils of personal relationships who feel no compulsion to hold up their end of any bargain they enter into. We're talking about otherwise honorable individuals who believe that everyone has an obligation to abide by the agreements into which they enter—everyone except, sometimes, them.

∾

My friend has asked for more time to repay me because she's working on her blog.

When a friend wants to change the deal

Question: I lent a college friend $1,650 so she could travel to Argentina to meet her boyfriend's family. Jessica agreed she'd pay me back in a year, but now that the year is up, she's asked for more time. She's taking a break from her job to concentrate on her blog, and she and her boyfriend, who can't work because he doesn't have the right visa, are strapped for cash. I'm sympathetic to Jessica, but I could really use the money. My partner and I just moved into our first home together, and we've been counting on the $1,650 to fix it up. Can I tell Jessica she must stick to our agreement?

Answer: Jessica has made a series of choices that have put her in a financial bind. This is her problem, not yours. If a misfortune had befallen her—had she been seriously injured in a traffic accident, for example—then she might reasonably ask you to extend the loan. But the only "misfortune" Jessica's experiencing is life in the real world—the world in which college-educated world travelers who choose not to work still have to meet their financial obligations.

If we sound harsh, it's because Jessica sounds like someone who's always going to believe she needs your money more than you do. First she needed it to travel. Now she needs it so she can focus on her blog. What will she need it for next, her IRA?

You've already shown great kindness by lending your friend $1,650 so that she could take a trip that presumably was important to her. Now you need the money for something that's equally important to you: your home. You're not morally obligated to extend the loan, and there's nothing unethical about asking Jessica to honor the commitment she made to repay it.

Our friends won't give us our deposit back.

When you're forced to bail on a joint vacation

Question: My wife and I arranged to rent a houseboat on Lake Powell for a week with friends who have kids about the same age as ours. Each family put up a nonrefundable $1,000 deposit toward the $4,000 fee. Then, a couple of days before we were to leave, my father died unexpectedly, and we had to cancel our trip. Our friends went anyway, though.

Of course we don't blame them for going ahead with their vacation. But the problem is, they haven't offered to repay us for the $1,000 deposit we lost. My wife and I feel that, since our friends got the benefit of having the entire houseboat to themselves, they should pay the entire bill. Are we wrong?

Answer: Yes. In fact, you've gotten off easy.

Imagine that your friends hadn't been able to go without you because, say, they couldn't afford to pay the balance of the houseboat rental plus all the gas on their own. Under those circumstances, they could make a pretty good case for why you should reimburse *them* for the $1,000 deposit they were forced to forfeit because you were unable to go.

Indeed, even having taken the trip, your friends wouldn't be out of line in expecting you to pay half of the balance due on the houseboat had your reason for canceling been anything less serious than a death in the family. After all, they built their vacation plans and budget around a deal you'd agreed to, and that deal called for you to pay $2,000—not $1,000—toward the houseboat rental.

In a perfect world, your friends would have found another family to go on the trip with them, and those folks could have compensated you for your lost deposit. But the world's imperfect, and the odds are low of finding a second family you'd care to live on a boat with who are also available on short notice for a specific seven-day stretch.

We're very sorry that you lost your father and sorry, as well, that his untimely death necessitated your walking away from a $1,000 nonrefundable deposit. But any way you look at it, his death cost your friends $1,000, as well. While they owe you their sympathy and support on your father's passing, they most certainly don't owe you a thousand bucks.

Standing the Test of Time

You've seen it in the movies a hundred times. Some talented young performers get together, start an act or maybe a band, and solemnly swear to stay together forever.

That's Act One. In Act Two, a showbiz heavyweight comes along and offers the most talented member of the group a career-making opportunity—but only if that person will leave the others behind. And one way or another, the star-to-be always ends up taking the deal.

If you think these movies have nothing in common with your life, think again. For example, imagine that you and your next-door neighbor finally have a little time now that your children are going to preschool. Since you're a pretty good jewelry-maker and she's got a background in marketing, the two of you decide to start a small business in which you'll make the jewelry and she'll promote and sell it. Maybe everything works out, and the business provides each of you with both the creative outlet and the income you'd hoped for.

Or maybe, just when the business seems to be taking off, your neighbor tells you that the perfect part-time job has opened up with her old employer and she really can't wait to go back to work. Like the star-to-be who abandons her colleagues, your neighbor feels a little bad about walking away from the business—but not bad enough to pass up the opportunity that's come her way.

Or picture this: You have a brother who has a couple of kids about the same age as yours, and he comes to you with this proposal: "Let's buy a small place on the water together that we can take turns using in the summer. It's a good investment, and it'll be great for the kids."

Maybe the two of you buy it, and all goes well. Or maybe you buy it, and a year or so later, your brother says he'd like to sell the place so he and his family can start traveling, the fact that you and your family continue to enjoy it notwithstanding. In other words, like the star-to-be who wants to move on, your brother finds the agreement he made with you to be constraining, and he wants out.

Are these folks behaving ethically? Yes and no. A deal is a deal—not a temporary arrangement we're free to walk away from the moment a better opportunity or more attractive alternative presents itself. But deals like these, with friends and relatives, generally include the unspoken proviso that you'll each try to accommodate the other's needs should circumstances change. And it's this proviso that the people who want out inevitably interpret to mean that they're doing nothing wrong in bailing.

Rock star, neighbor, or brother, it all boils down to this: No matter how honorable and well-intentioned the person you're dealing with is, you shouldn't count on a long-term, but only loosely specified deal holding together should it cease to provide your partner with the benefits it once did. For the fact is, most people are unwilling to make big sacrifices in order to honor a commitment made at some point in the past—especially if, from the perspective of the deal-breaker, circumstances have changed.

Does this mean it's a bad idea to count on friends and family to stick to a deal? Not necessarily. But it's a good idea to be prepared to be flexible—because that's what they're going to expect you to be if their needs change.

✎— CONTRACTS VERSUS HANDSHAKES —✎

When's a deal not a deal? When paper and ink are not involved. At least that's what almost half of survey respondents seemed to feel when we asked them whether they agreed or disagreed that "A deal is not a deal unless it's written down."

Here are their responses:

PERCENT WHO ANSWERED

Agree	44%
Disagree	56%

Source: Fleming & Schwarz survey.

In fact, the law says that oral agreements are as binding as written ones (it's just more difficult to prove their existence). And ethics is at one with the law: As a matter of honor, a handshake should be every bit as binding as a signature. As a practical matter, though, don't be terribly surprised if someone fails to honor an oral commitment *and* feels they've done nothing wrong. Unfortunately, most people agree with Samuel Goldwyn, who famously remarked, "An oral agreement's not worth the paper it's printed on."

Must I drop out of law school to repay my friend?

When friends want their money back before a loan is due

Question: Two years ago, when I was stuck in a dead-end job, I decided to go to law school. To do this, I had to work nights, and I almost didn't make it through my first year with all the demands of school and the job. I was seriously thinking of not returning the second year when my old boyfriend Richard, with whom I've remained friends, offered to lend me $20,000 so I could cut back on my job and concentrate on school. He works for Google and has made a lot of money, and he said I could pay him back once I graduated, passed the bar, and got going financially. I accepted, and thanks to the loan, my second year in law school was a whole lot better.

That was a year ago. Now—three weeks before the fall semester of my final year is set to begin—Richard has called and told me that he and his fiancée are trying to get the money together to make a down payment on a home and that he'd appreciate it if I would repay as much of his loan as I can. I still have $10,000 of his in the bank that I was counting on for my final year. Must I give it back? I'm not sure that I can make it through school if I have to go back to working thirty hours a week.

Answer: Normally it's the borrower who needs to be reminded that a deal is a deal and that you don't get to reschedule a loan payment just because the agreed-upon due date has become inconvenient. But the same holds true for lenders. A deal is still a deal. Since Richard is not facing any sort of dire emergency or misfortune—and since, we assume, you have not come into an inheritance or some other financial windfall—it would be unreasonable for him to insist that you repay him early (though it was perfectly reasonable for him to ask if you could). After all, he promised you could use the money to complete law school.

But that said, Richard did you an enormous favor in lending you $20,000, and you are obligated to try to accommodate him in return. This doesn't mean you must give him the $10,000 you have in the bank and either drop out of law school or take a job that makes life and school unbearable. But it does mean seeing if you can't find another party to lend you all or part of the $10,000 (the whole $20,000 would be better). Perhaps there's a student loan program for which you qualify. Perhaps there's a bank willing to make a bet on a soon-to-be member of the bar. You owe it to Richard to try—really try—to borrow the money elsewhere, even though the terms of the loan won't be as good. But you don't owe it to Richard to return the $10,000 if you can't.

ᖇ— PLAYING BY THE RULES: AGE MATTERS —᙭

Imagine that you and your family buy a home in a new development that has a homeowners association. After moving in, you paint your front door and window frames a new color that looks great with the color of the exterior of the house.

(continued)

You then get a notice from the homeowners association telling you that their bylaws require you to use one of ten specific colors when you paint the trim on your home. While you knew there were bylaws intended to maintain the appearance of the community, you hadn't realized that the color of paint was regulated. In this situation, how you would feel?

That's the question we put to participants in our survey, and here are the answers they had to choose from:

- The homeowners association is crazy. Sure, they have to see that everybody keeps their homes looking nice. But my home does look nice—the color we chose is fine, and we shouldn't have to obey some silly paint rule.

- I think our home looks fine, but I realize the rules have to be enforced. If the homeowners association starts making exceptions, then everyone will expect to do as they please. Besides, we knew there were rules when we moved in, and if we decide we don't like them, we can always move.

Here's how the participants responded, divided in terms of those under the age of forty and those forty and older.

PERCENT WHO ANSWERED	UNDER AGE 40	40 AND OLDER
Homeowners association is crazy.	43%	23%
The rules have to be enforced.	57%	77%

Source: Fleming & Schwarz survey.   *(continued)*

Why the dramatic difference in the two age groups? We suspect it's because the older you are, the more likely experience has taught you that when rules designed to maintain a degree of decorum are waived or treated as optional, the least decorous take it as license to do as they please. Specifically, you understand that, in the scenario above, the moment the paint rule is not enforced, another homeowner is going to feel free to use a bedspread for a window curtain or invite his in-laws to spend July in their RV in front of his house. And when the homeowners association tells these folks that they're breaking the rules, they're going to say, "But you let the guy across the street paint his shutters gray, and that's against the rules, too."

Does the data also imply that young people are less ethical? Not really. But it does imply that a substantial minority of them are unbecomingly clueless about a fact of life, namely: People expect you to honor the agreements you enter into, regardless of whether you think some aspects of the deal are so trivial they shouldn't matter.

Why should my friend's other creditors get paid before me?

How hard should you press people to honor their commitment to repay you?

Question: My father, a widower, has become good friends with a young couple in his apartment building who are very nice to him. They frequently pick up groceries for him, they often invite him over to watch a movie, and they have him to dinner now and then. My father reciprocates by taking them out for a meal once in a while and buying their boys DVDs, computer games, and the like.

About a year ago, the husband, Matt, told me he was in a tight spot and asked if I could lend him $4,500, promising to pay me back $300 per month. I was happy to help him out, and he was very appreciative. But he's been very bad about repaying the loan. In all, I've received eight of the twelve payments I should have gotten by now, and I had to call and ask him for most of those.

Recently Matt's wife confided to my father that Matt had lost a lot of money speculating in commodities and that they'd had to take out a high-interest loan to stay out of bankruptcy. From what she said, I can see that the only way I'm going to get the rest of my money back is to pester Matt each month, and I feel bad about doing this. But I can also see that the less I get, the more the finance company and his other creditors are going to get. As sympathetic as I am to the position Matt's in, I don't see why I should be at the back of the line. What do you think? Would it be wrong to continue to ask him for the money when he fails to make his monthly payment?

Answer: Matt and his family have been very nice to your father, and the loan you gave them was a kindness in return. Your benevolence will mean a lot more, however, if you can afford to cut Matt some slack in repaying you. He and his family are in a jam here—a jam of his own making, to be sure, but a jam nevertheless. You'd be doing them a great

favor if you could tell Matt to forget about repaying you until he gets back on his feet. His family is providing your father with something invaluable—company and attention. Here's your chance to repay them with a comparable good deed, namely: lessening the pressure they're under at a particularly difficult time.

My rich uncle is angry because I paid him back a little late.

When someone insists a deal must be honored word-for-word

Question: A while back I borrowed some money from my aunt and uncle to buy a Laundromat. They insisted that I pay them back a certain amount every month. When they went to stay with their older daughter in San Diego for the summer, I was supposed to drop the checks off with their son, Armando, who stayed behind to study for his advanced placement exams.

After they left, I had some unexpected expenses. So because my aunt and uncle have plenty of money and I knew they didn't need my cash, I told Armando that I'd have the June, July, and August checks to him before his folks returned—which I did—and I asked him not say anything about their being a little late. But Armando told his parents, and now my aunt and uncle are furious at me. They got their money, so what's their problem?

Answer: Let's see: You tried to take advantage of your cousin's youth. You asked him to betray his parents' trust.

You failed to uphold your end of your deal with your aunt and uncle. And you're wondering why they're angry?

Sure, your aunt and uncle ultimately wound up with the cash they were owed. And sure, the cost to them of the delay was small. But the principle is big: They trusted you when they lent you that money, and you welshed on your agreement to repay it. What's more, you tried to hide what you were doing.

All of us would like to be able to change the terms of an agreement when it suits us. But as Yogi Berra might say, if the deal hasn't been honored, you haven't honored the deal. You didn't keep your word, they're mad, and they have a right to be.

Chapter Sixteen

The Wedding Bill Blues

Another bride. Another June. Another sunny
honeymoon.

—Gus Kahn ("Makin' Whoopie")

WHEN IT COMES to the tensions that can be created by the intersection of money and relationships, a wedding has all the ingredients for a perfect storm.

To begin with, weddings are expensive. The average price tag is close to $30,000 these days.

Then, of course, two families are involved—families who may scarcely know each other and who frequently have very different tastes, expectations, and bank accounts. Even when people are on their best behavior, there are sure to be bumps in the road—if not potholes.

Finally, there are all the wedding guests for whom the nuptials also are anything but a free ride. There's an episode of *Sex in the City* in which Carrie estimates she spent well over $2,000 on one couple's wedding, including a shower present, a wedding present, clothes for the wedding, and a round trip to Maine, where the wedding was held. And, of course, she still worries that the bride and groom thought she went cheap on their gifts.

It's a good thing a wedding is a joyous event. Otherwise people might get the wrong idea.

~

My parents are too practical to give me the wedding I want.

When parents won't pay for a fancy wedding

Question: I'm twenty-four years old, and I've always dreamed of having a big, fancy wedding. But my parents are refusing to pay for one. I'm getting married next spring, and they want to give Wilson and me a small wedding plus $25,000 to put toward the down payment on our first house. They say we'll be better off with a big wedding present than a big wedding.

Do I really have to give in on this? I know it's their money, but it will be my memories. Wilson says either way is fine with him, but I feel so sad when I go to my friends' wonderful weddings and think that I'll never have this.

Answer: Money makes the mare go, as your great-grandparents used to say.

We're sorry you're not getting the wedding you'd always

hoped for, but you're right about one thing: It *is* your parents' money, which means they get to call the shots. And you can scarcely call them tightwads. Twenty-five grand is quite a wedding present.

None of which is to say that you can't have the wedding of your dreams. You can. But to do so, you and Wilson are going to have to make up the difference between your parents' budget and the wedding's cost.

True, you may have to postpone the wedding while you save up the money for it, and true, that will mean scrimping for a while. But when it's your money, you get to call the shots. And then you can have a wedding that is as lavish and romantic as the one you've always dreamed of.

Being a bridesmaid is killing me.

When a member of the wedding party wants out

Question: The maid of honor for a destination wedding in which I'll be a bridesmaid has organized an elaborate shower for the bride. She expects me and the other bridesmaids to share the cost of this expensive event, even though I won't be attending. (I can't afford the airfare to go to both this bash and the wedding.) Must I pay a share of the expenses for a party I'm not going to have anything to do with?

Answer: Some folks just love to spend other people's money.

You are under no ethical obligation to pay for a party you

won't be attending and about whose planning and cost you weren't consulted. Unless, that is, you agreed in the first place to cohost it. So: Did the maid of honor simply spring this soiree on you? Or is it possible that, in asking you to be in her wedding, the bride assumed you knew that one of your responsibilities would be to help give a party for her—a duty, we would add, that often goes with being a bridesmaid?

If the answer to the latter question is yes, we're afraid you're stuck. You can explain to the maid of honor that the party she's planned is too expensive for your budget and propose a more modest event. You can lead an uprising of the bridesmaids and oust the maid of honor as the party planner-in-chief. You can even ask the bride to intercede. But you can't walk away from the bill without walking away from an obligation—and, in doing so, sticking the other bridesmaids with your share of the tab.

᳉— IS THIS A WEDDING OR A FUND-RAISER? —᳉

Imagine that you're going to the wedding of a couple in their forties. Because they already have all the household items they need, they have asked that—rather than bring gifts—guests make a donation to a nonprofit organization that champions political causes you strongly oppose. Would you make a donation?

That's the question we asked the participants in our survey, and here are their responses:

(continued)

PERCENT WHO SAY

Definitely make a donation.	4.5%
Probably make a donation.	20.0%
Not make a donation, because you can't stand the politics of the organization.	55.0%
Not make a donation, because you believe your friends are wrong to ask for a donation instead of a wedding present.	3.5%
Not make a donation, both because you can't stand the politics of the organization and because you believe your friends are wrong to ask for a donation.	17.0%

Source: Fleming & Schwarz survey.

As you can see, three out of four people are unwilling to indulge the naïveté or arrogance of friends foolish enough to use their wedding as an opportunity to celebrate their political views—at least when the people don't share the happy couple's politics. As believers that there is no virtue in being a pushover when someone makes an unreasonable request for your money, we applaud them. And we have a suggestion if this ever happens to you: Identify an organization whose mission you and the bride and groom all approve of, and make a donation to it in their names.

My wife got stuck with a big hospital bill
when she was a teenager, and now a collection service is
coming after me.

When the bride brings debts to the marriage

Question: Five years ago, before we were married, my wife had to have emergency medical care at a local hospital. Amber was eighteen at the time, and she thought her step-father's insurance covered her. But it turned out not to, and the hospital says she owes them $15,000. Her credit has been destroyed by this debt, which the hospital has now turned over to a collection agency. And when Amber and I got married, they started coming after me, too.

Do you agree that we shouldn't have to pay for something that happened when Amber was a kid? It's not like she meant to run up this bill.

Answer: You have our sympathy. It's tough to start married life under the burden of a $15,000 debt. But the fact is, it's the hospital that's the victim here, not you. They provided Amber with emergency medical services, and five years later they still haven't been paid. To be sure, Amber thought her stepfather's health insurance covered her. But that was Amber's mistake, not the hospital's, and it doesn't justify stiffing them. We hate to tell you this, but it's time to take your medicine and begin paying off the debt.

⌒— ISN'T IT ROMANTIC? —⌒

Conventional wisdom has it that women are more romantic while men are more pragmatic. We're not sure if this particular paradigm ever was actually valid. But in any case, the results of our survey show that it's women who are more likely to be the pragmatists at one very important juncture in life. Consider:

We asked survey participants whether or not they agreed with the statement: "You should never marry someone who is deeply in debt no matter how much you love them."

Here—by gender—are their responses:

	MALE	FEMALE
Percent who agree	30%	48%
Percent who disagree	70%	52%

Source: Fleming & Schwarz survey.

As Michael Corleone would say, "It's not personal. It's strictly business."

How can I find a bride when I'm broke?

Money and courtship

Question: My longtime girlfriend and I split up a few months ago, and I am now starting to date again, with marriage and, ultimately, a family in mind. What concerns me is that the women I go out with may form a false impression of how much money I have. I am forty-two years old, I live in a nice condo, I drive a luxury car, and I have a good job in the beverage industry. But back in the dot-com days I started an Internet-based wine distribution business that went bankrupt and left me just about broke. I rent my condo, I lease my car, I owe my parents $50,000, and the balance in my IRA is sixty-two cents. I do, however, have a good income and so can pay for the nice meals, the concert tickets, and the weekend getaways that dating involves. But I know that, in doing so, I project an aura of prosperity that is entirely false. At what point in a relationship must I reveal my true financial situation?

Answer: You certainly don't need to make the balance in your IRA the centerpiece of your eHarmony or Match.com profile. But when you do meet someone in whom your interest is more than casual, you should tell her as soon as possible where you stand. Not only is it unethical to allow the person you're dating to develop a false impression of you, it's also counterproductive. After all, if you wait until after a romance has blossomed to reveal your true situation, the woman of your dreams may stop thinking of you as Prince Charming and start thinking of you as a manipulative little frog who pulled a bait-and-switch.

To be sure, courtship always involves some bait-and-switching. But projecting the rosy glow of prosperity when you're so far in the hole is a much more serious deception than, say, faking an interest in chick flicks.

⌒— TRUTH IN DATING —⌒

Imagine you're the guy who wrote the last letter. When would you reveal your financial position to the women you go out with?

That's the question we asked half the participants in our survey. The other half were told to imagine that they were a woman in the same position and asked when they felt they should acknowledge that they were broke.

What's the verdict? Roughly one person in three thought you should speak up no later than when you know you're interested in someone, while about 40 percent felt you should wait until you know your interest is returned.

As reasonable as waiting until you know the feelings are mutual sounds, the fact is, it means you're allowing the person you're dating to become interested in someone who's not the real you. As we pointed out in answering the last letter, not only is this unethical, it runs the risk of costing you the person you care for when they learn the truth.

Exactly what percentage of men and what percentage of women believe you should speak up at different points in courtship—from the time you first go out together to the time you first sleep together to the time you get married (and all the stops in between)? That data is listed in the tables that follow. We'll leave you to draw your own conclusions about the information they contain—facts such as:

- Almost one out of ten men think a man has no obligation to reveal that he's broke, even after the wedding;

- For most people, sleeping together is not a crucial juncture in the relationship as far as the obligation to reveal your financial status goes; and

(continued)

- Both men and women are a good bit more likely to believe that a woman should wait until she's sure her interest is returned before revealing her financial status than to believe that men should hold out that long.

⌁ WHEN TO RAISE THAT AWKWARD SUBJECT ⌁

Scenario A: You're a MAN who is broke, and you're dating with marriage in mind.

PERCENT WHO SAY YOU SHOULD REVEAL
YOUR FINANCIAL STATUS AT EACH STAGE

	MEN	WOMEN
In your online dating profile.	2%	4%
The first time you go out together.	6%	6%
As soon as you know you're interested in her.	26%	28%
As soon as you know your interest in her is returned.	40%	36%
Before you sleep together.	5%	3%
Only if you decide to move in together.	6%	13%
Only if you decide to get married.	7%	9%
Only after the wedding.	0%	0%
Never—your finances are your own business.	8%	1%

(continued)

Scenario B: You're a WOMAN who is broke, and you're dating with marriage in mind.

PERCENT WHO SAY YOU SHOULD REVEAL
YOUR FINANCIAL STATUS AT EACH STAGE

	MEN	WOMEN
In your online dating profile.	4%	0%
The first time you go out together.	4%	7%
As soon as you know you're interested in him.	17%	15%
As soon as you know your interest in him is returned.	42%	36%
Before you sleep together.	5%	8%
Only if you decide to move in together.	19%	16%
Only if you decide to get married.	7%	12%
Only after the wedding.	0%	1%
Never—your finances are your own business.	2%	5%

Source: Fleming & Schwarz survey.

The wedding's off, but my daughter won't return our money.

When the wedding is postponed

Question: Earlier this year, our thirty-four-year-old daughter told my ex-husband Randy and me that she and her boyfriend were planning to get married in December. Brigid has never been married before, and she wanted a big wedding. So she gave us a budget, and Randy and I agreed to split the expenses. Now Brigid tells us that she and Patrick have postponed the wedding and that no new date has been set.

I believe this wedding is never going to happen because I can see Patrick's gotten cold feet. I've asked Brigid to return the money Randy and I gave her, less any nonrefundable deposits and so on, but she's refused. Am I wrong to want my money back? This is causing a big rift in my current family.

Answer: Sounds like you get the picture better than your daughter does.

Since a new date hasn't been set for the wedding, your daughter should honor your request and return what remains of the money you gave her. Just because Brigid is more optimistic than you are about her chances of marrying Patrick doesn't mean she is free to hold your money hostage to her hopes.

Should they put a new date in the calendar—in ink— the happy couple can again ask you and your ex for financial help. And if they do, think about paying your share of the bills for the wedding as they come in, rather than giving your daughter a lump sum in advance.

What, Me Worry?
GIFT-GIVING ANXIETY

Feeling a little concerned about selecting the appropriate wedding present for your neighbors' daughter's wedding? You're not alone. Do a Google search for "gift-giving anxiety," and about a quarter of a million items turn up. There are postings on the Web sites of mental health organizations with headlines such as "How to Combat Gift-Giving Anxiety." There are podcasts of sermons with titles such as "Beat the Gift-Giving Anxiety Syndrome through the Tool of True Giving." There are an endless number of newspaper articles and guidebooks on the subject. And there are some very insightful articles written by psychologists and other social scientists who've become interested in the topic.

What the academics have to say is this: Gift-giving anxiety is rooted in a desire to make a good impression—a desire not simply to please the gift's recipient, but to be perceived as someone sophisticated enough to give just the gift the occasion calls for. In other words, it's our awareness or belief that the recipient's opinion of us will be shaped by the gift, combined with our uncertainty about how our gift will be perceived, that leads us to worry. Call it an identity crisis (though psychologists wouldn't). When we're experiencing gift-giving anxiety, what we're really worrying about is how we're identifying ourselves to the people we're buying the gift for.

Happily, most of the gifts we buy are for friends and

relatives who know us well—well enough that we aren't worried that any one gift is going to shape their opinion of us. Plus most of the gifts we give are for birthdays and holidays—annual events for which conventions have become established. That's why we don't spend a lot of time worrying that our brother or sister is going to think of us as socially inferior because of the birthday presents we choose.

But when it's a wedding—when the boss's daughter is getting married and you feel it's imperative to give her the perfect gift; when your best friend is marrying and you want to give her something genuinely special; when your college roommate's daughter, whom you've never met, is getting married and you'd like to send her a gift that telegraphs to her father just how much his friendship has meant to you—welcome to the world of gift-giving anxiety.

In brief: Take a very special event, add expectations that are less than clear, and throw in a person whose impression of you you care very much about. What do you get? Another example of how weddings have all the ingredients for a perfect storm—and a good reason why gift registries are so popular.

Okay. So these are Tony Soprano's problems, not yours. But they could be. For while the Sopranos are not your typical American family, the money-and-relationships issues Tony faces are—as the list above suggests—not all that different from the issues that all of us struggle with at one time or another.

What follows are some of the problems that have confronted other, less exotic families—in particular, the problems with their parents that drive kids crazy and the problems with their kids that drive parents crazy.

～

Our grown sons are living off us.

When adult children move back home

Question: We have two children living at home. One is thirty-one years old and the other is thirty-three. Both of our sons have been married, and both are now divorced. Are we crazy to think that they should be kicking in for utilities, groceries, and the like? While they are forced to pay quite a bit in alimony and child support, both boys have good jobs. My wife and I are retired now, and while we don't want to charge rent, we don't think it would hurt them to help out. Your opinion would be most appreciated.

Answer: We're afraid to ask how long the boys have been bunking with you.

Yes, your sons should be kicking in for household expenses. But that's the least of it. More fundamentally, they

Chapter Seventeen

Parents and Kids

⟶ ✦ ⟵

Remember—as far as anyone knows, we're a nice, normal family.

—Homer Simpson

YOUR MOTHER IS furious at you for putting her in a nursing home and suspects your real agenda is to take her house and sell it. Your sister is resentful that you ended up with the family business and is never satisfied with the share of the profits you give her. Your brother-in-law is a bit of a bumbler, but you keep him on the payroll out of loyalty to your sister, even though she's not appreciative. Your wife complains that you're never around, but she certainly enjoys the money you bring in and the jewelry you bring home. And then there's your son. Instead of inheriting your ambition, the lazy kid seems to have inherited only his mother's affinity for spending.

should be acting like adults. That means paying their own way in life, not mooching off their parents. This is true for twenty-somethings, and it goes double for men in their thirties with good jobs. And while we hate to blame the victim, you bear some responsibility for allowing them to behave so selfishly.

Fortunately it's never too late for tough love. Now is the time to present your sons with a bill for living expenses, including rent. And don't take "no can do" for an answer.

✎— BOOMERANG BABIES —✎

PERCENT OF ADULTS IN EACH AGE GROUP
WHO LIVE WITH THEIR PARENTS

22–24 year olds	60%
25–29 year olds	30%
30–34 year olds	25%

Since when have developers been putting basketball courts in retirement communities? Since retirees' adult children began moving back in with them, a phenomenon that began in the 1990s. (These children are twice as likely to be male, hence the basketball courts, rather than, say, nail salons.)

Source: Armin Brott, WomenOf.com.

(continued)

> Do these parents and their adult children ever disagree about who is going to pay for what? You bet. It happens all the time.
>
> So what's fair? What's fair is what the parents think is fair. If the kids don't like the deal, they can always do what they were dying to do as teenagers: Move out.

My mother is stiffing my kids.

When an adult child resents the financial help
a parent gives his sister's family

Question: I have two children, my sister one. Recently, my mother has begun "helping" with my niece's expenses. First it was clothes, then a computer, then one-on-one tutoring. Meanwhile, Mom has never offered my wife and me any help with our kids. While it's true we make more than my sister and brother-in-law, they're not what anyone would call "needy"—and we have more kids to support. Isn't my mother being unfair?

Answer: Not necessarily. While parents have a moral obligation to not play favorites with their children as they grow up, things are a little different for grandparents. In particular, it's not unusual—or wrong—for a grandparent to become closer to one grandchild than another. Sometimes the reason is proximity, sometimes it's temperament, sometimes it's the amount of attention the grandchild gives them.

There's no rule that says every grandchild must be treated exactly the same when the relationships are different. And there is also no rule that requires your mother to give your family money just because she's given money to your sister's family. While we can understand your annoyance if Sis is playing the poor-relation card, the fact remains that the money at issue belongs to your mother and is by and large hers to do with as she wishes.

This said, your mother does have an obligation to not slight your children and to not signal to them that she favors your sister's child. While she's free to spend more money on your niece and to devote more attention to her, your mother shouldn't be volunteering to your kids that she's doing more for her other grandchild—and neither should you.

ᎧᎨ MUST PARENTS GIVE EQUALLY TO THEIR CHILDREN? ᎨᎧ

The sentiments expressed in the last letter are hardly unique. Everyone has an opinion on how Mom should be handing out her money, and, of course, not everyone shares the same perspective. Our research for *Money* shows that **two out of three people believe you should never give a large gift of money to one of your adult children unless you give the same amount to all of the others**. While that's a sizable majority, it's not an overwhelming one. Which means that whatever Mom decides to do with her money, there's a reasonably good chance that someone in the family is going to think she's wrong.

⌒— **EVERY FAMILY HAS ONE** —⌒

Eight out of ten people agree that in most families, there's
always one person who's always complaining about not
having enough money—even if it's not true.

Source: Fleming & Schwarz survey.

My fifteen-year-old is a piker.

When your kids want you to pay for things
they can afford to buy themselves

Question: Our fifteen-year-old son is always asking us to pay
for the things he wants: spiffy sneakers, a new video game,
a better bicycle. What troubles us is that he never wants to
spend any of his own money on these things. His grandparents and other relatives often give him nice checks on
his birthday and on holidays, and we give him an allowance. But Brandon squirrels all this money away and expects us to pay for everything. We don't want to discourage
our son from saving, but we think this is wrong. Do you
agree, or should we just be grateful that he doesn't blow his
money on junk the way most of his friends do?

Answer: We agree. It's time for Brandon to open his piggy
bank.

While your son clearly understands the virtues of saving his money, he obviously has failed to grasp the virtues

of spending it, instead of counting on others to provide him with the things he wants.

In other words, your Brandon has become a moocher-in-training—and you need to nip that in the bud!

NO ONE LOVES A MOOCH

Nine out of ten people say they'd rather have a brother-in-law who's a cheapskate than a brother-in-law who's a moocher.

Source: Fleming & Schwarz survey.

Is it fair to spend more on a gifted son than on his siblings?

When a talented child could benefit from expensive training

Question: We've been told our youngest child shows great promise as a pianist. Unfortunately, nurturing his talent—specifically, getting him a private tutor—is very expensive. My husband and I are prepared to make the sacrifices this will take, but what about our other two children? Is it fair to devote a disproportionate share of our family's resources to one child, knowing his sisters will get cheaper and fewer bikes, computers, and so on, as a result?

Answer: Being fair to your children doesn't require you to spend the same amount on each of them. But if you're planning to devote considerably more of the family's resources to one child, you need to be certain there will be enough money left for some of the activities that interest the other two, even though they may be less gifted and even if the activities that interest them are less refined.

It's perfectly reasonable to lower your family's standard of living a little—to ratchet down the spending on family vacations, say, or to require your children to get an extra year or two out of their bikes and computers—all to help offset the cost of the tutor. But what isn't fair is to design a budget that includes piano lessons for your youngest child but that requires you, for example, to deny his older sister the two weeks of basketball camp she's been longing for.

In short, while there is nothing wrong about spending more on one child than another, you shouldn't set aside the wants and needs of your other children in the process. Good luck in achieving this delicate balance.

My son doesn't want me to get a divorce because he'll be hurt financially.

When an adult child pressures you to stay married

Question: My marriage has been rocky for a long time, and I've finally decided to leave my husband, Gary. When I confided this to my son, Will, he urged me to reconsider. Will says that if I leave Gary, Gary is sure to stop using Will as his stockbroker. Will's right about this—Gary's been giving our business to our son mainly at my insistence. We are by far Will's largest account, and I know Gary believes that

Will would be better off making it on his own. I've lasted this long with Gary, so I guess I could manage to continue for Will's sake, but I'd really rather not. What is my obligation to Will in this situation?

Answer: Your obligation to your son was to feed him, shelter him, educate him, and teach him right from wrong—all while he was a minor. But now that Will is a grown-up, you have no obligation to stay in an unhappy marriage so that he can maintain the charade of being financially independent. You should decide whether to divorce Gary based on the merits of your marriage, not on the basis of your son's selfish request that you put his bank account ahead of your happiness.

   Not that you shouldn't help Will out if he needs it. You should. But we agree with Gary. You're not doing your son a favor by supporting him in a job at which he apparently would be failing—or forced to work a whole lot harder—were it not for the patronage of his parents.

ᨁ— THE LESSER OF TWO EVILS —ᨁ

Three out of four people say they would rather have a grown child who's a tightwad than a grown child who's a spendthrift.

Source: Fleming & Schwarz survey.

I'd like to help my parents out,
but I don't think I can.

When elderly parents ask for help you can't
afford to give

Question: My parents, who have been hardworking people all their lives, are getting ready to retire. They live in Indiana, but they would like to move to Arizona, where the weather is better. The problem is, houses down there cost a lot more than what my parents can hope to get for their home. So they've asked me if I can help them out. While I'd really like to and my wife would as well, we simply can't. We have two children, and most months there's nothing left from our paychecks after we pay the bills. We have a small savings account, but that's our rainy day fund. What should we do?

Answer: From what you say, there's not much you can do. Your obligation to your wife and children trumps your obligation to your parents. If your mother or father needed money for a medical emergency, that would be one thing. But their desire to move—as understandable and reasonable as it is—is not sufficient reason for you to put your own family at risk by depleting your modest savings.

Even so, we hope you'll take a close look at your budget and see if there's not some way you can squeeze out, say, $150 per month to send your parents. That's enough to cover at least $25,000 of mortgage debt, which ought to help them some. Or they could rent a nicer place if they knew they could count on you for help with the rent.

But if you can't afford it, you can't afford it. And making a commitment you cannot keep would certainly not be doing your parents a favor.

Chapter Eighteen

Cheating on the Friendship

⁓

It is easier to wage war with wise enemies than be at
peace with foolish friends.

—Afghan proverb

Friends who live two time zones away and with whom you
are no longer close invite you to the wedding of a daughter
you've never met, knowing you won't go but that you can be
counted on to send a nice gift.

An old friend from college asks to spend a couple of nights
on your couch while she interviews for a job in the area,
then stays for ten days, using your apartment as a free hotel
while she visits other friends.

And the couple with whom you and your husband take a
golf vacation every year never fail to grab the best bedroom

in the homes and condos you rent together when you travel.

THERE'S A NAME for this kind of chutzpah: It's called "cheating on the friendship."

And there's always a new twist. Today you have to hope that, when you're invited to a dinner party at your friends' home, your hosts don't announce, as they're serving dessert, that the purpose of the dinner is to support a cause that is dear to their hearts—then pass around a bowl for donations (and pledges are most welcome if you didn't happen to bring your checkbook).

People who cheat on friendships are not dishonest or selfish, at least not in the conventional sense. Ask them to hold your watch, and you know you'll get it back. Ask them to pick up a load of groceries when your family's come down with the flu, and they're off to the store. They're nice folks.

Which is what makes the problems we experience with them so vexing: they're *good* people. But, alas—like us—they're not perfect.

∼

I'm paying for their porterhouse, and they're paying for my pasta.

When your friends order more—a lot more

Question: Ten of us go out to dinner after work once or twice a week, always splitting the tab equally. At a recent meal, eight people ordered entrees that cost twelve to fourteen dollars, while two ordered twenty-two-dollar steaks. When the check arrived, the steak eaters said nothing about paying a larger share of the bill. I know the amounts aren't huge, but shouldn't they have offered to pay nine dollars or so more than the rest of us?

Answer: Absolutely. People split checks not only because it's gracious and convenient, but because they're operating on the premise that over time things even out. For that to work, though, the differences in the cost of the meals have to be relatively small—not the 50 percent gap you report. So unless the two steak eaters have been consistently ordering cheaper meals than the rest of you while paying a full share, they should have covered the extra cost of their much pricier dinners.

As for their silence when the check arrived, there are three kinds of people who don't seem to notice they've run up a much higher tab than everyone else: the freeloaders, the clueless, and those who just can't do the math. Whatever accounts for your colleagues' behavior, you can always ask them to chip in more money if they don't volunteer. In fact, if this happens again, you should. Assuming they weren't freeloading, they'll appreciate the reminder. And if they were counting on their coworkers to keep subsidizing their steaks, they'll realize the deal is off.

⟿ UNSTUCK WITH THE TAB ⟿

Suppose that you and your spouse frequently go out to dinner with another couple and always split the check. Recently, though, the couple has begun ordering meals and drinks that are significantly more expensive than yours. What would you do?

That's the question we asked the participants in our survey, and one in ten said they wouldn't do anything because they wouldn't mind paying for half the tab. Here's what those who did mind said they would do:

PERCENT WHO ANSWERED

Nothing. I don't like to confront people about things like this.	3%
Start ordering more expensive meals and drinks ourselves in order to even things out.	16%
Say nothing, but stop going out with them or go out with them less frequently.	18%
Hint to them that perhaps each couple should pay for what they ordered.	29%
Ask them to pay an amount that reflected how much more expensive their meals and drinks were.	34%

Source: Fleming & Schwarz survey.

If you feel like having lobster with friends who always order chicken, offer to kick in more when the check arrives. Nine times out of ten, you'll be making someone happy—not to mention doing the right thing.

The clothes my friend is trying to sell me are awful.

When a close friend expects your business

Question: My good friend Carolyn recently left the large law firm where both she and her husband have long been partners to open a clothing boutique where she sells her own designs. Now, every time I see her, Carolyn twists my arm to shop there.

Is she wrong to press me to buy her expensive creations, which happen to look hideous on me? While I can afford them, I don't want a closetful of clothes I'll never wear.

Answer: So that explains all those alarming-looking unworn garments at second-time-around shops.

There is certainly nothing unethical about trying to sell things to friends. Who better, after all, to buy a budding artist's first painting or to be a real estate agent's first client?

So it's not unreasonable for Carolyn to urge you to visit her shop. Nor would she be wrong to expect you to attend her gala opening, to encourage your friends to visit her store, and to be generally supportive of her new venture. But what isn't right is for Carolyn to push her clothing so relentlessly that you feel uncomfortable saying no. Putting you in that position—whether she's flogging a five-hundred-dollar sweater or a five-dollar raffle ticket—is not just rude, it's taking unfair advantage of your friendship.

Then there's the fact that Carolyn obviously isn't strapped for cash. While we all have an obligation to help out our friends, this doesn't mean you have to turn a blind

eye to their overall financial situation—especially when they want you to buy something you don't want, need, or care for. So unless you've been leaning on Carolyn to buy a table at your favorite charity's annual fund-raiser or she's been bringing business to your catering service—unless there's some quid pro quo here—you're under no obligation to get out your checkbook for your prosperous pal.

How can our friends be so selfish with their vacation home?

When a good friend says no to a request

Question: Our good friends own a vacation home where we've been their guests many summers. Recently we asked them if our family could occasionally use the house for ski weekends in the winter, when they're rarely there. Although we promised to pay our share of the utilities and take good care of things, they said no. Are we wrong to feel they've betrayed our friendship?

Answer: Pay your share of the utilities? Come on! How'd you like it if someone assumed your car was available whenever you weren't using it and felt virtuous for offering to replace the gas. Kids might think that way, but adults have an obligation to understand what cars—and second homes—really cost to operate.

Look, there's a basic principle you've lost sight of: Yes, everyone has a right to expect generosity from their friends. But we don't have the right to dictate the terms of that gen-

erosity. Your friends have, for many summers, made you welcome at their place. Whatever their reasons were for declining to provide your family with a free ski cabin—privacy, wear and tear, or perhaps the nuisance and expense of having to arrange for someone to plow the driveway—they've done nothing wrong. So take it easy: You haven't been betrayed.

—◦ UNWELCOME HOUSEGUESTS ◦—

We've all run into this problem at one time or another: Out-of-town friends call and ask if they can stay with you for a day or two while they're in your area. You say fine, they arrive, and, a week later, they still haven't left. What do you do?

That's what we asked the participants in our survey. About one out of five said they'd do nothing because they wouldn't care how long their houseguest hung around.

And what about the four out of five who wanted the guest to leave? Here's what they said they'd do:

PERCENT WHO ANSWERED

Nothing. I don't like to confront people about things like this.	6%
Hint to them that I'd like them to leave.	35%
Ask them to leave, making up an excuse (that's a lie) for why they can't stay.	16%
Ask them to leave without making up an excuse.	43%

Source: Fleming & Schwarz survey.

(*continued*)

As you can see, only 43 percent of the respondents who wanted the houseguest to go said they'd feel comfortable being direct and asking their friend to leave. The other 57 percent said they'd either do nothing or beat around the bush in one way or another.

No one likes confrontation. But it's not difficult to see why freeloaders have so little difficulty exploiting others when, as these results show, over half their victims are unwilling to look them in the eye and tell them the party's over.

My friend never seems to have any cash with her.

When someone you know is always short ten or twenty bucks

Question: My good friend Claire has a very annoying habit: She never has any cash with her when we go out. She never has cash for the movies, she never has cash for drinks, she never has cash for coffee. Wherever we go, I wind up paying, and she promises to pay me back. Occasionally she remembers to do so, but most of the time I have to ask, and often I just let it go.

Claire's a good person otherwise. Am I being petty in letting the money stuff bother me? And any suggestions for what I can do about this?

Answer: You're not being petty. One of the responsibilities that comes with being an adult is taking enough money with you when you go out to pay your own way. Another is recognizing that regularly hitting your friends up for cash is an imposition. Being a good friend in other ways doesn't get Claire off the hook on these points. She needs to grow up and stop behaving like a child.

To move her in the right direction, you might try bringing less money when the two of you go out and explaining to Claire that you have only enough for your own drinks or movie ticket. But then what? Presumably you don't want to go to the movies alone.

The truth is, it's unlikely you can solve this problem without being direct with Claire—without pointing out what she's been doing and asking her to change. If you're unwilling to do this, you're left with two choices: being Claire's twenty-four-hour cash machine or no longer hanging out with her. Good luck in working this out.

⌒— **YES, THERE IS A SANTA CLAUS** —⌒

One out of eight people say that when they lend someone ten or twenty bucks, they don't expect to be repaid.

Source: Fleming & Schwarz survey.

Our freeloading friends are driving us crazy.

Isn't it *their* turn to pick up the check?

Question: For the past several years, my wife and I have been going out to dinner once or twice a month with another couple. Until recently we all had staff jobs at the local state college, but six months ago I quit to work in the private sector. Now that I'm making a lot more money, our friends always seem to expect us to pick up the check.

These friends are not struggling financially. They own their own home, take nice vacations, and have much more time than I do to pursue their not inexpensive hobbies. Not only that, the college provides them with wonderful benefits. In short, our friends can well afford to continue to pay for their share of the meals we eat out together.

Am I right to be angry? Or, given the disparity in our incomes, should my wife and I be picking up the checks and not complaining?

Answer: We understand this happens to Bill Gates whenever he goes out to dinner with Steve Jobs, and it's getting old for him, too.

Seriously, your friends have apparently decided that they know exactly how altruistic your new level of income requires you to be. And while they probably wouldn't phrase it quite this way, their philosophy seems to be that the successful should subsidize the quite comfortable, at least when the quite comfortable means them.

Now don't get us wrong. Generosity is a great virtue, and treating your friends to dinner would be a nice thing for you to do—and for them to reciprocate—from time to time. But the virtues of generosity notwithstanding, your friends are out of line in assuming that your now heftier paycheck entitles them to a free meal whenever the four of you go out.

So unless you and your wife have been insisting on

going to more expensive restaurants or have begun ordering more expensive wine—unless, in short, you're responsible for a substantial increase in the cost of the dinners—you may with a clear conscience ask your friends to split the check.

⌒— SPLITTING THE CHECK —⌒

One out of three people agree that when friends go out to dinner, someone is always unhappy with how the check is divided.

Source: Fleming & Schwarz survey.

Chapter Nineteen

Living with the
Thieves of Kindness

― ✦ ―

You can be as romantic as you please about love,
Hector, but you mustn't be romantic about money.
—George Bernard Shaw,
Man and Superman

WHAT WOULD WE do without our friends and family? After looking through this book, a smart alec might answer, "Sleep better."

To recap, here are just a few of the survey results we've reported:

- Eighty-seven percent of the public say that every family has at least one person who tries to get more than his or her share after a relative dies.

- Seventy-nine percent say that lending money to someone is a good way to ruin a friendship.

- Seventy-five percent say it is common for people to lie, cheat, or pretend to be loving in order to be in someone's will.

- Sixty-eight percent say they've experienced trouble with friends or family members in the process of borrowing or lending money.

- Sixty percent say they have at least one friend or relative who's a "user," meaning a person who takes advantage of other people. And

- Only 34 percent say they never have problems involving money with close friends or relatives.

In light of this data, it's not surprising that when we asked the participants in our survey if they felt they were too generous with others, two-thirds said they were. What this says is that most people are good-hearted to a fault . . . but not necessarily by design. Because what we know from the surveys we've conducted and the letters we receive is that most folks are both unhappy and resentful when the loans they make are not repaid, when a guest moves in and refuses to move out, and when their selfish siblings help themselves to their parents' treasures. While forgiving an unpaid loan or housing an unwanted guest may be an act of generosity, it also is often an act of surrender—an occasion where an ethically-challenged person has taken advantage of a kind and loyal one.

In the popular '80s sitcom *Family Ties*, Michael J. Fox played Alex P. Keaton, the conservative son of two quintessentially '60s liberals. In one episode, the preschool that Alex's younger brother Andy attends asks each child to come to school wearing a small sign on his or her chest—a sign that reflects something the child takes pride in. And so the children come to school wearing signs that say things like "I have two sisters," "My hamster's name is Midgie," and "I can count to eleven." Andy's sign is a little different, however. Thanks to his brother Alex, Andy's sign says "I know what's mine."

You needn't share Alex Keaton's politics to appreciate the virtue of that sign. As the previous pages have shown, the world is filled with people who either don't know what isn't theirs or don't worry about what's yours.

So what can you do about them? Start by removing the sign your mother pinned on you when you went to nursery school—the one that says "I love to share, and I'm not confrontational." Admirable as these two qualities are, the thieves of kindness in this world read that sign to say "I am a doormat."

Which isn't to say you shouldn't share. Of course you should. But when to share is up to you, not to the folks who believe you always have an obligation to accommodate their needs.

And of course you don't want to spend your life confronting people. But now and then, that's exactly what you must do. Nothing enables a thief of kindness like someone who refuses to take exception to the theft.

So by all means be generous and be kind, but don't be a pushover. Remember Charles Barkley's on-the-mark advice to LeBron James: "Learn to say no." And remember, there's nothing wrong with saying, when the occasion calls for it, "Isn't it *your* turn to pick up the check?"

Do you have a question you would like the authors to answer?

Contact them at:
FlemingandSchwarz@MoneyandEthics.net

Note on the Surveys

The *Money* survey the authors refer to is a nationwide on-line survey with one thousand respondents that was conducted by *Money Magazine*. The survey was designed and analyzed for *Money* by the authors, Jeanne Fleming, Ph.D., and Leonard Schwarz. Data collection was carried out in February/March 2007 by The Research Spectrum. The survey has a sampling error of plus or minus 3.1 percent. Some questions were asked of only half the sample. These items have a sampling error of plus or minus 4.1 percent.

The authors themselves conducted a separate study, the Fleming & Schwarz survey. The Fleming & Schwarz survey is a nationwide online survey with eight hundred respondents. It was designed, conducted, and analyzed by the authors. The survey has a sampling error of 3.5 percent. Some questions were asked of only half the sample, and these items have a sampling error of 4.9 percent. Data collection for this survey was carried out in March 2007 by Polimetrix.

Acknowledgments

Without the generous encouragement of Diane Harris, Michael Hiestand, Bill Sharpe, Eric Schurenberg, Jason Zweig, and the late William Woo, we never would have had an opportunity to write this book. At crucial points in bringing it to fruition, Harriet Chessman and David Denby provided invaluable advice and perspective. Finally, first-time authors should all be so fortunate as to have someone as wise as Susan Golomb as their agent and as creative as Emily Loose as their editor. To these kind people, as well as to all the friends and family members who have been so supportive, we extend our heartfelt gratitude.

ABOUT THE AUTHORS

Jeanne Fleming, Ph.D., and **Leonard Schwarz** are the authors of "Do the Right Thing," a column on money and ethics in *Money* and a blog with the same name that is featured on CNNMoney.com. They make their home in Palo Alto, California.